Praise for

The Five-Star Church

★ ★ ★ ★ ★

The Five-Star Church is packed with principles, ideas
and strategies that will strengthen the leadership and effectiveness
of any church with a future-focused ministry.

DR. BOB BROWER
PRESIDENT, POINT LOMA NAZARENE UNIVERSITY
POINT LOMA, CALIFORNIA

Being a successful church today means that you do
everything possible to serve people to the glory of God—whatever
your size, wherever you are. *The Five-Star Church* is a practical
instruction manual that will help you implement quality
control of the highest level in your ministry.

DALE E. GALLOWAY
DEAN, BEESON INTERNATIONAL CENTER, ASBURY SEMINARY
WILMORE, KENTUCKY

The Five-Star Church hits the bulls-eye! Successful, steadily growing
local churches are the benchmark of every city that has been
measurably impacted by the gospel in our generation. Because of
this, the twenty-first-century revival will not be a short-term event,
but rather an extended process of winning and discipling people
through local churches. This is now a textbook for every employee
on my church staff. These ideas work. This book is great!

TED HAGGARD
SENIOR PASTOR, NEW LIFE CHURCH
COLORADO SPRINGS, COLORADO

Praise for

The Five-Star Church

★ ★ ★ ★ ★

Stan Toler and Alan Nelson have written a creative resource for
pastors and congregations striving for excellence. *The Five-Star Church*
will be a powerful instrument for leading the Church to a higher
quality of ministry in meeting the needs of God's people.

BISHOP JAMES D. LEGGETT
GENERAL SUPERINTENDENT,
INTERNATIONAL PENTECOSTAL HOLINESS CHURCH

Christians have permitted a subtle deception to take root in the
Church today: the acceptance of mediocrity. We build our places of
worship, operate our ministry events and cultivate our spiritual
lives with little thought given to the rigorous pursuit of quality in
the name of Jesus. Now there is a clarion call for believers to
embrace the high calling of excellence—*The Five-Star Church*.
This book is long overdue and sorely needed.

DR. JOHN C. MAXWELL
FOUNDER, THE INJOY GROUP
ATLANTA, GEORGIA

From the perspective of forty-nine years in the ministry,
I strongly recommend this long overdue book.
It is a behind-the-scenes, innovative, whatever-it-takes approach to
developing a congregation geared to meet today's demands for
excellence. The authors' message is a must for churches truly
seeking to be used of the Lord in a contemporary way.

DR. PAUL L. WALKER
GENERAL OVERSEER, CHURCH OF GOD
CLEVELAND, TENNESSEE

the Five ★★★★★ Star

CHURCH

HELPING YOUR CHURCH PROVIDE
THE HIGHEST LEVEL OF SERVICE
TO GOD AND HIS PEOPLE

STAN | ALAN
TOLER | NELSON

Regal

A Division of Gospel Light
Ventura, California, U.S.A.

Published by Regal Books
A Division of Gospel Light
Ventura, California, U.S.A.
Printed in U.S.A.

Regal Books is a ministry of Gospel Light, an evangelical Christian publisher dedicated to serving the local church. We believe God's vision for Gospel Light is to provide church leaders with biblical, user-friendly materials that will help them evangelize, disciple and minister to children, youth and families.

It is our prayer that this Regal book will help you discover biblical truth for your own life and help you meet the needs of others. May God richly bless you.

For a free catalog of resources from Regal Books and Gospel Light please call your Christian supplier, or contact us at 1-800-4-GOSPEL *or at* www.gospellight.com.

Cover Design by Kevin Keller
Interior Design by Robert Williams
Edited by Mike Yorkey and Wil Simon

Library of Congress Cataloging-in-Publication Data
Nelson, Alan E.
The five-star church : developing a church people love to
attend / Alan Nelson and Stan Toler.
p. cm.
ISBN 0-8307-2323-4 (hardcover)
1. Church management. I. Toler, Stan. II. Title.
BV652.N45   1999   98-55783
254—dc21   CIP

1 2 3 4 5 6 7 8 9 10 11 12 13 14 15 / 05 04 03 02 01 00 99

Rights for publishing this book in other languages are contracted by Gospel Literature International (GLINT). GLINT also provides technical help for the adaptation, translation and publishing of Bible study resources and books in scores of languages worldwide. For further information, write to GLINT at P.O. Box 4060, Ontario, CA 91761-1003, U.S.A. You may also send e-mail to Glintint@aol.com, or visit their web site at www.glint.org

*To the excellent people of Scottsdale Family Church,
who are quality minded and committed to growing
their souls. I love attending and pastoring their church.*

—ALAN NELSON

★

*To the Trinity Church of the Nazarene family.
Thanks for pursuing excellence with me as partners
in ministry. You are loved!*

—STAN TOLER

Contents

★ ★ ★ ★ ★

Foreword by Elmer Towns 9

Acknowledgments 11

Introduction 13

Chapter 1:   The People-Focused Church 15

Chapter 2:   Deming Comes to Church 33

Chapter 3:   My Utmost for His Highest 59

Chapter 4:   Excellence as a Process 81

Chapter 5:   Developing Quality Teams 97

Chapter 6:   Developing Team Members and Leaders 109

Chapter 7:   The Secret Church Shopper 125

Chapter 8:   Evaluation and Measurement 139

Chapter 9:   Sweat the Small Stuff: Attention to Detail,
             Efficiency and Effectiveness 161

Chapter 10: Quality in the Physical Arena 179

Chapter 11: Quality in the Program Arena 193

Chapter 12: Quality in the Spiritual Arena 209

Chapter 13: The Learning Church 219

APPENDICES

Appendix A: The Secret Church Shopper Survey 227

Appendix B: Church Rating Survey 231

Appendix C: A.C.T.S. (Action/Contact Tracking System) Form ... 235

Appendix D: Sample Agreements 237

Foreword

✭ ✭ ✭ ✭ ✭

The experience of staying overnight in a five-star hotel is vastly different from bedding down in an inexpensive motel. When you enter a five-star establishment, you discover a world of state of the-art facilities and unparalleled service. The management, ambiance, customer service and dining must be worthy of meriting five stars—the highest rating—for superior service in attitude, accommodations and resources. In a five-star hotel the customer is sure to get undisturbed rest. The result is a morning where you wake up invigorated, refreshed, and ready to tackle anything in the best possible fashion.

In a church environment, people should also look for quality and promote excellence in fellowship functions, building designs, and spiritual lives. They should search for and encourage a congregation to be a five-star church—a body that seeks excellence for the Lord in every endeavor.

Some churches have outstanding preaching, but they do very little in pastoral care for their members. Other churches have outstanding facilities and a lovely worship atmosphere but the sermon is weak and the teaching shallow. When these churches fall short of excellence that is honorable before God, we should ask: *In our love for the Lord, how do we find and build a church that has a quality mind-set in all areas of fellowship?*

Stan Toler and Alan Nelson have written *The Five-Star Church* to answer such a question. In this book, they encourage and provoke Christians to nurture hearts and minds devoted to excellence in our service for God. *The Five-Star Church* gives believers the criteria for a well-rounded ministry that is rooted in biblical standards and that provides quality service for all who attend.

The authors begin by sharing how the five-star church must be people-focused, bible-based and doctrinal-purposed. Next, Toler and Nelson show how a five-star church must always be centered on Jesus Christ and complemented with a pragmatic freedom within ministry (reaching a multitude of people, confronting various problems, and creating numerous solutions). The authors tell us that the five-star church must change lives, yet at the same time have an outstanding quality of worship, and do an outstanding job of teaching the Word of God.

Most books today target one or two aspects of ministry, but *The Five-Star Church* covers all the bases. This book helps church leaders to understand in a contemporary tell-it-like-it-is style about how to build balanced ministries in every area of New Testament responsibilities. The authors point out that "Jesus shows us a more excellent way." They want the Church to follow His example by consistently providing the best planning, labor and thought behind each ministry.

Both Stan Toler and Alan Nelson have planted churches. Both men have pastored large churches. At the present time, Alan Nelson pastors Scottsdale Family Church in Arizona, a congregation he was instrumental in starting which now has over 500 in attendance. Stan Toler has pastored three different megachurches in America. Currently, he is the Model Church Instructor of INJOY Ministries, teaching seminars weekly to pastors while also pastoring Trinity Nazarene Church in Oklahoma City, Oklahoma.

May God help us learn from their experience. May we learn to build more five-star churches to the glory of God.

Elmer Towns

Special thanks...
To Bill Greig III, Kyle Duncan, Kim Bangs
and the Regal Books family for making
***The Five-Star Church** a reality.*

★

To Deloris Leonard, Jeanne Griffin and
Carol Tillotson for their excellent
editorial assistance.

Introduction

✯ ✯ ✯ ✯ ✯

The Five-Star Church is a book designed to assist leaders in providing a ministry of excellence to everyone.

Each chapter consists of four sections:

1. A narrative portion, providing a running story of church leaders' learning points of excellence from a five-star hotel manager.
2. The Gist of It..., an explanation section, providing both principles and applications.
3. A question and answer section, which focuses on questions the leader is most likely to ask. (We actually answer them!)
4. A Doers Section, which proposes ideas for implementation and includes questions to assist the readers in analyzing their local church situation.

The attitude of the book tends toward a more contemporary approach to ministry. It is a no-fluff, tell-it-like-it-is approach that is uncommon among church-development books. Some might view it as irreverent, but we'll take the happy majority who are apt to find it very relevant. Discussing bad breath and dirty laundry aren't always pleasant, but it's a reality of life. View this book as a ministry Listerine commercial.

Yours for excellence in ministry,
Alan Nelson and Stan Toler

The People-Focused Church

★ ★ ★ ★ ★

There is no better exercise for strengthening the
heart than reaching down and lifting people up.

—LAWRENCE B. HICKS

The grounds were immaculate as the car wound up the curving drive toward the magnificent hotel entrance of Majesty Suites.

Looks like the palace of a king, Gary Carter thought, as he pulled into the parking lot. *Man! Some people have such a great place to work.* Gary stepped out of his car.

"Hey, nice place here," a friendly woman said. Gary turned around to see Beth Langley walking toward him—the director of Ministry Involvement at the church he pastored.

"Yeah, I agree," Gary responded, laughing. "How are you doing, Beth?"

"Just great! I love this hotel. What's on the agenda today?"

"I'm glad you got my message," Gary replied. "Jeff Hollister has been coming to Family Church for a few weeks. He's the general manager of Majesty Suites. I mentioned to him how impressed I was with the hotel and Capers restaurant, so he invited us to lunch."

"Great!"

Gary and Beth walked under the canopy of the pristine hotel entrance. An enthusiastic doorman held the door open and greeted them, "Good morning, folks! Welcome to Majesty Suites. Good to see you again, sir! We're glad you're here. If you need directions, let me know."

"Thank you," Gary responded. "I think we know where we're going."

"This place is amazing," Beth noted. "Everything is so well done, and everyone is so courteous and responsive to your needs."

Gary and Beth walked through the beautiful lobby of Majesty Suites. The air bustled with activity as people checked in and out. "This is a hopping place," Gary commented. "I've never been here when there was not some type of convention or activity going on. Capers restaurant and the coffee shop are pretty popular, too."

Gary and Beth walked up to a hostess. She smiled at them as they approached. "Good morning. Lunch for two today?"

"Good morning," Gary responded, looking at the hostess's name badge. "Jill, we're supposed to meet Mr. Hollister."

"Oh, yes, I was told that he was expecting you, Mr. Carter," the hostess explained. "Mr. Hollister had to take a call, but told me to give you our best table. He will be with you in a few minutes."

"Thanks," Gary replied.

Jill led them to a secluded table that overlooked an outdoor garden area. "Your waiter will be right with you."

Within moments, the waiter came around. The young man took Gary and Beth's order for two soft drinks just as Jeff Hollister, the hotel general manager, walked up to their table. "Gary, Beth, welcome to our humble abode. Thanks so much for coming."

Gary laughed, "Hey, when you offer a pastor a free lunch in his favorite restaurant, it's no big deal."

"Good to see you, Beth," Jeff said. "We've not gotten to talk much, but I've admired your ministry at Family Church."

"Thanks," Beth smiled. "I think I remember meeting your wife and children a couple of weeks ago. They are so sweet."

"Jennifer is the greatest, and so are the kids. I'm blessed."

"Jeff," Gary interjected, "I was telling Beth how busy this place is.

How do you keep so much business flowing in and out of Majesty Suites when so many hotels are struggling for business?"

"Majesty Suites is the only five-star hotel in the area," Jeff grinned, "so when people want a certain level of service and amenities, they pick us."

"They come because you're the only five-star hotel?" Beth asked.

"Really, we're the only five-star because people love coming here," Jeff laughed.

Gary was puzzled. "I don't get it."

"Well, obviously there are certain requirements for earning a five-star rating, but people don't return simply because of your rating. They come because you provide great service and constantly strive to meet their needs," Jeff explained.

"Hey," Beth lit up. "The classy music and chandeliers have to help."

"People might come once for a nice facility," Jeff continued, "but they keep coming back because they know that once they get here, they will be treated like kings and queens. We try to provide that little extra."

Gary noted, "So you mean that people don't just come for the marble and nice carpet. The marble, nice carpet and friendly people are all just expressions of meeting people's needs."

"That's right," Jeff nodded. "We started with the customers and built the hotel around them. Most places build the hotel first and then ask, 'How can we attract customers?' It's a mind-set."

Gary looked distantly at Jeff. "Would this work in the Church?"

"I don't see why not," Jeff answered. "People are people, regardless of the organization."

Beth commented, "Putting the customer first sounds so commercial—you know, corporate and market driven. Isn't our goal to put God first?"

"I don't see any conflict," Jeff said. "We are to put God first, but God was the One who told us to love and serve others, to meet their needs to the best of our ability. He's the One who sent Christ to die for us because He put our needs before His own."

"That's right," Gary said thoughtfully. "The Apostle Paul said, 'I have become all things to all men so that by all possible means I might save some'" (1 Cor. 9:22).

Beth wondered, "So we're not compromising on the gospel by putting people at the center of our ministry?"

"It's not an either-or, but a both-and situation," Jeff responded. Churches ought to be the leaders in excellence and customer service because we have the highest stakes—eternity."

Gary confessed, "Then why do so many churches eke out such a mediocre existence? Why do we think of ministry as a second-class activity? I know I'm new at Family Church, but right now, I'd have to rate us a two- or three-star."

"I guess it's priorities," Jeff said. "Five-star hotels like Majesty Suites are designed to make a profit. The best way to make a profit is to become all things to all people in order to win some. You don't have to be perfect, but you do need to strive for excellence."

"But why is the Church different?" Gary questioned. "We're not profit oriented, and the result seems that we're less responsive to change and excellence. But if we believe what we preach, we've got the most important message on earth."

"Amen," Jeff replied. "It kills me to see how hard we work to serve people in order to turn a profit, and how mediocre most churches are when their stakes are so much higher in the eternal scheme of things."

"Hey, the way a lot of churches do ministry is a joke," Gary observed. "I don't mean to be insensitive or disrespectful. I've seen enough ministries and talked to enough Christian business professionals, however, and there is no way they would stay in business if they ran their companies the way we run many of our churches."

"I think the idea of being market driven scares a lot of church people away," Jeff said. "Maybe a better term is being market sensitive or market oriented. After all, our goal is not to compromise the gospel and simply give people what they want. At Majesty Suites, we're in the hotel business. We don't fix cars, make house loans or train you how to run your computer. What we do, however, is provide for your meeting, eating and lodging needs. Within those parameters, we do all we can to personalize our service. A market-sensitive church need not compromise on its message, but it must change its methods if it is to meet the spiritual needs of people. Excuse my soapbox a second, but a market-oriented church gives people what they need in the way they like to receive it. Seems to me, that's what Jesus did most of the time."

"Still, doesn't it come down to money?" Beth suggested. "I mean, if we had these facilities and could hire and train quality staff, churches would be so much more effective."

"You don't have to have money to be a five-star person or organization," Jeff explained. "It's a mind-set. Money tends to flow with people, and people are attracted to organizations that are run with excellence and that are unabashedly committed to top-quality customer service."

"Excuses," Gary interrupted, staring into space. Beth and Jeff turned to him. "We in the Church are forever making excuses. We say we don't have the money. People aren't interested in spiritual things. Bottom line is that we don't have better churches and more quality ministry because we're not willing to pay the price. We've allowed the enemy to dupe us into believing that quality doesn't count, that sincerity is the only thing that does."

Beth and Jeff sat silently and watched as Gary's eyes brightened. "Uh, I've seen this look before," Beth commented. "He's about to have a brainstorm."

"We're going to become a five-star church!" After pausing briefly, Gary said, "Family Church is going to shake off the mentality that sincerity is all God wants. There is no reason in the world we should put up with mediocrity, just because we are a charitable organization. God deserves our best. You're right, Jeff. We have to put the customer first if we're going to obey God and bring glory to Him. We have to attract people to the Kingdom and help them find a better way in life."

"A five-star church," Jeff pondered. "I like that."

"I can see it now," Beth joked. "Next someone will come up with a directory of all faith communities in the area and rate them. Oh, here's a two-star church. We wouldn't be seen there. Let's check out the four-star congregation down the street."

"They do that anyway," Jeff explained. "People rate churches on how they are treated and by what they see, hear and feel. We don't publish it, but we tell our friends and neighbors. People keep coming back to Majesty Suites because the word is out—this is the place to be for quality service. We do very little outside marketing."

"And people will start coming to Family Church if we get the reputation of being a top-quality, service-oriented church in all we do," Gary said.

"They will," Jeff agreed.

"So what do we do to become a five-star church?" Beth asked.

"Jeff, would you help us? I've spent so much time in the Christian culture that I'm probably blind to many things that you take for granted in being customer focused. Would you be willing to meet with us every two or three weeks and help us implement what you've learned into Family Church?"

Jeff thought for a while. "I don't see why it wouldn't work. I've taken many courses and seminars in quality management and customer service for my work. Nearly all of it makes great sense for the Church because it's about relating to people."

"We would really appreciate it," Gary responded.

"It's a deal," Jeff said with a smile. "The five-star church has begun."

THE GIST OF IT...
WHY WE DO WHAT WE DO AND THE WAY WE DO IT

More than 80 percent of churches in the United States have plateaued or are declining. All it takes is a visit to these churches to understand why. They do not cater to the perceived needs of the community and are not aware of their lack of excellence. The self-image of the average congregation, as reflected in the signage, facilities, publicity, written materials and overall friendliness, reveals an inadequate self-esteem.

Quality "people care" does count. There are two primary reasons and two secondary reasons for this.

We need to strive for excellence and care about our church property, programming and publicity because God deserves our best. We, as the local church, are His local franchise within a community. We represent Him. The Bible says that all Christians are to act as ambassadors, as liaisons between God and others. When we do things that reflect a shabby mind-set, we are certainly not representing Him well, because God does things with excellence. Look at creation. After everything was created, He looked at it and said, "It is good." When we offer mediocre music, have unfriendly ushers and ho-hum services, and then present ourselves as a reflection of God's love and character, we insult Him. (We'll talk more about this in chapter 2.)

The other big reason for pursuing an unabashed, people-oriented ministry is that God commanded us to go into the world and make disciples of everyone. If you haven't noticed, quality counts more now than it ever has in terms of attracting people and keeping them. When we scrimp on quality, we communicate our lack of seriousness about our subject. Capitalism, higher education, greater affluence and market competitiveness have all been influences to make people more discretionary in how they spend their time and money. This affects the Church because our mission—whether we choose to accept it or not—is to reach people.

The Great Commission requires us to do whatever we can to win some, obviously within the parameters of the gospel. We need to come to terms with what those parameters are. A desire to serve people must come from our love for God. Otherwise, it will be humanistic.

A secondary reason to emphasize a customer orientation is that people are motivated by quality care. One of the best ways to raise the level of church-attendee commitment is presenting an orientation of excellence. When we do things that are shoddy and less than the best, people are not motivated to become a part of it.

Another secondary reason to pursue a customer-oriented ministry mind-set is that without it, we are doomed to stay as we are, or worse, to fail. Although this may sound like the inverse of the first primary reason, the idea here has more to do with us as an organization than us as a spiritual mission. The bottom line is that as our culture changes, we must respond to its needs differently. If we do not, we will lose touch and eventually close our doors.

Every organization in the world is facing significant changes created by a multitude of influences. Although our inherent message must never change, our methods must. We cannot operate the way we did in the '50s, '70s or even the '90s. The twenty-first century is here, and we have to be concerned about consistent, regular change. A customer-service, market-oriented church will be constantly changing so that it will stay fresh, healthy and vibrant as an organization, as well as to its mission to honor God and reach people.

CHRIST FIRST, OTHERS A CLOSE SECOND

Recently, Nancy Nelson (Alan's wife) went to the local grocery store. She wanted to buy some postage stamps at the checkout stand—just as they had advertised. The clerk said she was out of stamps, but the customer-service desk would have some. She went to the service desk and asked to purchase stamps using her debit card.

The clerk responded, "I'm sorry. We're not equipped to take debit cards here. You'll have to go to the checkout clerk to do that."

"She sent me here because she was out of stamps," Nancy responded. "Can't you work together to let me buy stamps?"

"I'm sorry," the service-desk person responded. "We keep those departments separate."

That is just one example of dozens of ho-hum, "I'm really not here to serve you" attitudes prevalent in businesses. It seems amazing how some stores can stay in business given the service apathy they exhibit.

Top service organizations typically gain reputations for the "second mile" service they provide for people. Courtesy, follow-through, giving the benefit of the doubt and service with a smile characterize service-oriented companies.

Nordstrom, an upscale department store chain, is renowned for the way it make its customers feel like royalty. Southwest Airlines cut the frills out of flying to provide very competitive savings without cutting back on humor and friendliness.

We are talking about the Church, however. What does customer service mean in terms of God's business?

Jesus emphasized the importance of prioritizing others, second only to loving God with all our strength (see Mark 12:33). The way we love others is by serving them and meeting their needs.

If we believe the Bible teaches that we must serve others out of reverence for Christ, and that people are going to spend an eternity in hell without our winning them for the Kingdom, then we must continually improve our methodologies to save some. The Church is a service-oriented organization. We function to help people find relationships, answers, and to link up with appropriate resources. For us to develop an authentic customer-service orientation, we must understand who the customers are, what their needs are, and how they need to be served.

> Customers needed...no experience necessary!
> (Outdoor sign at the Sand Dollar restaurant
> in Venice, Florida)

To be customer-oriented means to be focused on meeting the needs of people.

—ALAN NELSON

IDENTIFYING POTENTIAL CUSTOMERS

Most churches are structured to provide ministries for those who are already inside the doors. Once a person ventures past the threshold a few times and appears to become a regular part of the church, then he or she is considered a customer, even though many might dislike this term.

Most churches serve only a couple of demographic groups. These churches are not large enough to have a lot of customer diversity because of their very size (70 to 150 members). People tend to seek out those who are like themselves, which is why we generally see like-minded people in a single congregation. These like-minded people naturally develop ministries around their interests, needs and priorities. When similar people visit the church, there is apt to be some sort of bonding. However, when people with varying tastes, needs or traditions attend, it is difficult for them to relate to one another; often, they move on.

The more a congregation considers its people customers, the more likely it is to develop a broader range of ministries to relate to varying needs, interests and priorities. Larger churches and those that seek to grow will develop events, programs and services that are able to attract more people.

The corporate comparison is like a department store compared to a single-item store. Identifying the needs of the people within a congregation will help determine what ministries need to be developed and also which ones need to end. Single parents, never-marrieds, youth, children, senior adults, recovering alcoholics and weekend athletes are but a few of the subgroups a congregation with a broad range of ministries may identify with. Taking on these ministries and creating a user-friendly, customer-oriented culture means a church is apt to have more of its existing people involved and committed.

Anyone who thinks the customer isn't important
should try doing without them for ninety days!

—STAN TOLER'S BARBER,
BOB SCHUBERT

EXECUTING THE EXCUSES

Someone once said, "An excuse is a reason wrapped up in a lie."
Jesus constantly dealt with the excuses of people for not following
Him. It's a disease of human nature. Why would any congregation
not assertively want to seek a service oriented ministry?

- "We're too busy doing what we're doing now to take on
  any new projects."
- "We don't have the staff or budget to do more."
- "We are up to here in meetings, events and program
  preparation."
- "New people might start coming to our church, and that
  would upset our delicate balance."
- "I like the way things are now."

The theme of most of these excuses relates to an underlying
problem of denial.

- "Things aren't that bad. Why do we need to improve?
  People still come."
- "The building looks fine to me."
- "Hey, if people want to know where the nursery is, they
  can ask."
- "We're a church, not some profit-driven organization;
  besides, God will understand."
- "We're a charitable, volunteer institution. People don't
  expect as much from us."

- "If it's okay for us, it's okay for everyone else."
- "If they don't like us the way we are, tough."

Although few would so boldly make these declarations, most churches communicate varying degrees of these denial statements. Some call it the Lake Wobegon syndrome: We think we are better than we really are.

If a church, parish or any faith community is intentionally going to pursue a serious look at becoming more customer oriented, the vision has to be cast by leaders. All pastors, priests and rectors are not necessarily leaders. Many are teachers, counselors and managers. If that is your case, then you will need to find lay leaders who possess the ability to cast the vision for a customer orientation.

Without this emphasis by leaders, you may as well quit. Close this book and stick it on your bookshelf until you have an idea of who might carry that burden. That may seem abrupt and even cynical, but unless those who have influence grasp the burden to develop a service-oriented church, it ain't gonna happen.

Nothing is changed by a mediocre performance.

—JOHN MAXWELL

QUESTIONS AND ANSWERS

Q. Help me deal with this: How can I truly be bent on pleasing God and be market sensitive and market oriented as well? In other words, if I give it to them in the way they want, won't I be compromising the gospel?

Alan: We don't want to just "tickle ears" and entertain as the means to an end. Rather, our goal is to give them what they need, but in a way they want. It's more like providing medicine in a chewable tablet form rather than by injection. The process by which we present the gospel is as important as the product.

Too often we emphasize the product, downplay the process, and then wonder why people are not coming to visit our church, or worse, not returning after they have visited. Jesus never had a canned approach to the good news. He was forever relating to people where they lived, and at times that meant going against the religious norms and practices of the day.

There is an old saying, but it fits: People don't care how much you know until they know how much you care. They don't know you care unless you respond to their perceived needs or their real needs in ways that are loving and accepting.

Q. Customer service is just secular, business-talk lingo for humanistic strategies. We're a faith community, not a hotel or department store.

Stan: Recently, I was traveling on American Airlines to Tampa, Florida. The flight was delayed because the flight attendants had not arrived in Dallas, Texas.

Surprisingly, the pilot began to serve drinks and peanuts to the frustrated passengers. One passenger asked the captain why he was doing the work of the attendants, and he said, "It's my job to keep everyone on this flight happy. Besides, haven't you seen the movie *Airplane?*" We all laughed heartily!

Later, I thought, *I wonder if the pastoral staff in most local churches would do what the pilot did in that situation?* Personally, I was challenged to watch for opportunities as a pastor to model customer service to parishioners.

Alan: One reason we use the term "customer service" is that when we talk about faith and love in the Church, sometimes we get really mushy and sentimental. It's tough to hit a target you can't see well. Customer service helps us better define and measure how we're doing. Besides, for-profit organizations are teaching us that zeal in serving others is a good way to reach people. There is no reason why we in the Church cannot learn from those who have different motivations. Most churches are not growing, because they have lost their concept of quality people care. Service is a very Christian concept, and the word "customer" is preferred because it gets us out of our ministry comfort zones. We are vendors of spiritual growth opportunities, like it or not.

Q. What do you do when your clients include those who have been in the church for years, and those who need to be in the church from the community? They seem to have different needs.

Stan: Not long ago, I was asked to speak to the Atlanta Hawks basketball team. Apparently, members of the team had been given a copy of my book *Minute Motivators*. Naturally, I invited my son Adam and my nephew Aaron to go with me to the game. We had great fun and a wonderful time of fellowship with the players.

Afterward, we ate at Planet Hollywood restaurant. What made this trip to the restaurant memorable was my stop at their rest room. You see, I have this policy of always going to the rest room before I eat! My view is this: *If the rest room is dirty, I'm not eating...if it's clean, I eat!*

To my amazement, when I walked into the Planet Hollywood rest room, a man greeted me as he sprayed air freshener around the room. He walked to the sink and turned on the water and dispensed soft soap into my hands. After I rinsed my hands, he handed me a white towel and offered a top-of-the-line cologne for me to use!

Then he pulled a comb from the sterilizer and gave me some styling spritzer. After that, he offered me a mint and invited me to come back soon. (After a few diet cokes...I was back!)

Talk about customer service! I immediately thought the Church could do a lot better in meeting and identifying potential attendees. For instance, at my church we designed and built a beautiful welcome center for our guests. After hearing me tell the Planet

Hollywood story, our ladies beautifully redesigned their rest room! (I still need to convince the men that it matters.)

> *Here is a simple but powerful rule: Always give*
> *people more than they expect to get.*
>
> — NELSON BOSWELL

Q. Give me some examples of bad service that I might be blind to in my own church.

Stan: Ernie Davenport, the CEO of Eastman Chemicals, tells the story of a businesswoman who stopped at a coffee shop and ordered a cup of coffee. The waitress grudgingly delivered it. She asked, "Anything else?"

"Yes," said the businesswoman. "I'd like some sugar, cream, a spoon, a napkin and a saucer for the cup."

"Well, aren't you the demanding one," snapped the waitress.

"Look at it from my point of view," said the businesswoman. "You served a cup of coffee and made five mistakes."

Recently I discovered several insights regarding the business community and customer service. The following observations reflect this discovery:

OBSERVATIONS ABOUT CUSTOMER SERVICE

1. Poor service is the number-one reason American companies lose business.
2. The average dissatisfied customer tells nine others of the dissatisfaction.
3. It costs between 5 and 10 times as much to attract a new customer as it does to keep an old one.
4. Excellence leads to increased sales.

Personally, I think bad service starts in the church parking lots. For example, one church I served had a serious parking problem. One Sunday just after I had arrived, a friend of mine came for a visit. After church he told me he had asked the parking lot attendant where he should park and was told, "Do the best you can!" Hardly what I had in mind about customer service.

Several months ago I had the privilege of attending the First Baptist Church of Orlando, Florida. I was impressed with their parking lot attendants and, most of all, with the piped worship music to the parking lot. Now, there is an example of good service!

Alan: You don't have to travel to many churches before you realize how few are really user friendly. From chipped paint to inadequate signage, from boring, dated worship services to dirty nurseries, we miss the way others perceive us.

A lack of communication about who we are and what we do may be one of the biggest blind spots. Who do I talk to for information? How can I get plugged into ministry involvement? Where do I take my infant? How do I find the first-grade class? Who are the pastors and lay staff members?

Don't assume everyone knows where the front door is, where the rest rooms are, or where the kids are supposed to go. Assumptions always create blind spots, and most churches assume far too much of those who are coming as visitors.

Satisfy the customer first, last and always.
— PETER DRUCKER

Q. So if we want to get serious about helping our church be more quality oriented and customer-service focused, what should we do?

Alan: Read the rest of this book.

Stan: Don't do it alone. It's too easy to pretend that one person can do this by himself (or herself). Get a group of people together, hopefully those who have some formal or informal influence and are willing to face some tough issues about your church and the ministries that might cause some discomfort.

If you can't find any of those kind of people, then start with anyone interested in improving the quality of the church and ministry. Use this book as a study-group guide and work through each chapter, one at a time, not progressing until you've acted on the Doers Section at the end of every chapter.

THE DOERS SECTION

We have to be bluntly honest with you. This book is intended to create some sparks. If you read it cover to cover without moments of frustration with the current status of your church or ministry, then you're not getting our point. The best churches are not perfect, but they are forever pursuing the ideal.

The purpose of The Doers Section is to help us avoid being hearers only and deceive ourselves into thinking that things are just fine the way they are in our faith community. We encourage you to use this section in a group format for the purpose of getting a variety of views and establishing an action plan to implement changes in your congregation.

QUESTIONS TO DISCUSS

- Who are the clients or customers of our church?
- What are the real and felt needs of these people?
- What are we doing to measure customer service in our church?
- What do we think we might be doing well? Poorly?
- What are some potential blind spots?
- What tools, instruments or feedback systems do we have in place?

- Can we stay true to the gospel and yet strive to meet the needs of people in a way that is attractive?
- What is the growth rate in our church in the last five years?
- What percentage of our guests are we retaining?
- What does this indicate regarding our service orientation?
- Who are the leaders in our church?
- With whom do we need to consult in order for us to become a quality, service-oriented church?

Each and every person in the church must understand his or her unique role in making ministry to guests happen.

— STAN TOLER

Deming Comes to Church

★ ★ ★ ★ ★

Jeff Hollister, general manager of the Majesty Suites Hotel, met Gary and Beth at the front desk.

"Good morning," he said with a smile.

"Good morning," Beth and Gary chimed in unison. "Thanks for hosting our first session of five-star training."

"No problem," Jeff responded. "I have to be honest. I'm pretty excited about reviewing these ideas for Family Church. Follow me. I've got a meeting room set up for us that will give us more privacy than the restaurant."

The three walked down the hall.

"I was sort of looking forward to the restaurant," Beth grinned. "I love the food here at Majesty Suites."

"Well, I think we can do something to accommodate that," said Jeff, as he swung open the door to a tastefully decorated meeting room. Against a far wall, a cold-cut buffet had been set up on a table, along with chilled soft drinks. Paper and pens were provided on top of a conference table which stood in the middle of the room. A nearby stand held a computer and video projector.

"You think of everything," Beth replied, "don't you, Jeff? I was just kidding about the lunch."

"We want to treat you well," Jeff explained. "After all, if we're talking about what makes a five-star organization, we can't be chintzy."

"We could," Gary chuckled.

"That's one of the myths we're going to work on changing," Jeff said. "Spending the little extra to go beyond what is expected goes a long way in making people feel special about the experience. It takes so little to be above average."

The three loaded their plates and sat at the conference table to eat and make small talk.

When the plates had been cleared, Jeff got down to business. "Today I thought we'd talk about some principles behind the quality movement," he began. "These principles will help us develop a mind-set for what we're going to be working on and talking about in subsequent meetings."

"Are you talking about the Deming and Quality Circle stuff?" Beth asked.

"Yes, that's part of it," Jeff responded.

Gary added, "Beth, you didn't get that in seminary, did you?"

"Unfortunately not." Beth explained, "Before coming to Family Church, I worked in a corporation that was discussing some of these things. We did some basic training on the concepts."

"Good," Jeff said. "The pursuit of excellence has strong theological support, but no one has captured the theory and development of it better in modern times than post-World War II capitalistic organizations. Probably the best-known early developer of incorporating excellence was a man named W. Edwards Deming. His teachings initially didn't receive much response from American industry because we thought we were doing fine without it. The Japanese, who were hungry for ideas that would help them come back from the war's devastation, embraced his teachings."

"Sounds like church life, turning down ideas that help us compete better in the marketplace," Gary suggested.

"That's human nature. Most of us are closed to new ideas when we think we are doing everything okay," Jeff explained. "But times have changed. Most of us remember when something made in Japan was junk. But then Sony, Toyota, Toshiba and Honda began showing up in every home in America with quality items. All of a sudden, we began reconsidering some of the ideas we'd rejected in the past. We started getting beaten at the bank."

Gary asked, "What is it going to take to get us ready for the changes you're about to propose?"

"I'm not going to propose any specific changes," Jeff said. "I'm just here to help our church understand and think about implementing a quality, ministry mind-set. Before any changes take place, there needs to be some sense of dissatisfaction with the status quo, along with a realization of a better way of doing things."

"That will be part of our challenge and responsibility," Beth added. "I think that too often churches are the last to catch on to progressive ideas, because our bottom line is less measurable."

"I agree with you," Jeff affirmed. "Motivation to change is a part of the leadership and implementation strategy, but first, let me give you a fast overview of the movement that spawned some of the principles we're going to be applying to Family Church."

Jeff handed Gary and Beth an outline and flipped on a laptop computer next to the conference table. A colored chart matching their handouts projected onto the wall.

"You've done your homework," Gary smiled.

"All of us will need to if we're going to take this seriously," Jeff explained.

The handout was titled, "Deming Comes to Church," and it listed 14 principles. "What I've done here is take Deming's 14 main principles and translate them into the context of a local congregation like Family Church. Here's Principle One," he said.

Principle One:
We want to be the best we can be, reach our potential, serve people better and glorify God. To do this, we must be intentional and perpetual.

Beth asked, "What does it mean?"

"It means innovation, research and education, continuous improvement, and even the maintenance of equipment, furnishings and facilities reflect who we are and what we do," said Jeff.

"It's the idea that we have to improve every aspect of our ministry" Gary noted, "to create a mind-set of excellence."

"You've got it," Jeff answered. "And there will always be room for improvement."

"But when you first explained it, it sounded so corporate," said Gary.

"At first," Jeff replied, "some of these may seem corporate because it is a foreign culture to many faith communities. But when you illustrate each point in the context of the local church, you'll see how natural the points are for us. Here's Principle Two." Everyone looked to the overhead.

Principle Two:
Let's practice what we preach and put thorns in our laurels.

Gary asked, "What does the 'thorns in our laurels' mean?"

"I borrowed that phrase from James Collins's book *Built to Last*," Jeff explained. "The book looks at what makes the difference between organizations that survive and thrive over the years as compared to those that just keep the doors open.

"One point of human nature is that we tend to rest on our laurels—accomplishments of the past. For example, we may claim to be a friendly church or to value evangelism, but where is the accountability? We need to build in ways that make us aware when we really don't measure up to our claims. By putting thorns in our laurels, we learn not to rest on them. Just because a church has been effective in the past doesn't mean it will be that way in the present or future."

Jeff continued with Principle Three:

Principle Three:
Everyone on the ministry team is involved in analyzing what we do, how we do it and how we can do it better to serve people best.

"Our goal is to make everyone who is involved in leading and working in a ministry to be part of the function for quality inspection," Jeff explained. "It shouldn't be up to the pastoral staff or just the ministry director to make sure we focus on improvement."

Beth surmised, "An equivalent to that might be the idea of getting an entire church body sharing its faith versus hiring a pastor of evangelism to make sure we witness."

"I think that's a very good illustration," Jeff nodded approvingly. "The idea is that unless we all take responsibility for keeping a look out for quality and areas of improvement, it's not likely to happen."

Gary added, "So we want people to be somewhat self-sufficient and motivated to do their own improvement rather than rely on some foreman-type minister?"

"Right," Jeff acknowledged. "It also means that annual reviews are dinosaurs. Weekly discussions on 'How did it go?' will become the norm. Part of putting together an event is not just the planning beforehand. Discussing how it went is just as valuable as planning how to do it. From now on, after an event is finished and memories are fresh, we should garner feedback. We should ask questions: What should we do differently next time? How can we improve? Do we want to do this again?"

"That really makes sense," Beth affirmed. "What's Principle Four?"

Principle Four:
Who are the best people for the ministry tasks, and what are the best resources we can afford?

"In the corporate realm," Jeff said, "a lot of lesser, quality-minded groups tend to award contracts primarily on price alone, instead of looking for other factors that enhance excellence. The church version is what we talked about in our first meeting. Just because we're a nonprofit organization doesn't mean we need to do everything in the cheapest way possible."

"I agree," responded Gary, "but that's going to be a tough idea to sell to some people. I agree that we need to be good stewards, but some people don't understand that stewardship is using their resources to the best of their ability. Sometimes, the cheapest way is not the best way."

"Exactly," Beth affirmed. "You can save a dollar here and there but end up looking cheap, shoddy and second rate. The problem is that there are so many opinions on what quality is, and when Grandma Brown tithes her Social Security check, you don't want to give the appearance of being a spendthrift."

"One of the biggest mistakes I see churches make is that they confuse stewardship with cheapness," said Jeff. "Often the two are opposites. Financial stewardship is about getting the most possible for your investment. The man who turned 5 talents into 10 received the highest commendations."

"You're right on," Gary chimed in. "What I hear you saying is that if we adopt a continual quality-improvement mind-set, we have to take into account quality issues in our facilities, services and equipment because quality is a good investment."

"I think that also has to do with the 'warm body syndrome' we see in ministry," said Beth. "Too many times, churches are just looking for a warm body to fill a ministry position instead of teaching people about their gifts and talents."

"We could use our new ministry gifts and profile database here to help us better determine the right person for the right role," Gary said. "I think sometimes we don't get the best people because we undersell a task, hoping to make it easier for prospective candidates to say yes."

Jeff affirmed, "You two are doing a great job translating this into Family Church's context. Yes, our congregation needs to find a place for everyone who is willing to serve, but just because people are willing does not necessarily qualify them for a certain ministry role."

"We'll have fun trying to implement Principle Four," Gary smiled.

"Good," said Jeff. "Let's look at Principle Five."

Principle Five:
We need to discuss the Q (quality) factor when we plan a project, after an event and in our scheduled staff meetings.

"First of all, this has to do with the depth of your commitment," Jeff began. "You, as paid staff, must buy into this, but for ministry excellence to become a meaningful part of Family Church, it must be accepted and implemented by everyone involved.

"Second, constant improvement must be intentional. The goal is not just meeting some preapproved standard, because that doesn't help us go further to provide better service. The need is to develop a method for initiating regular improvements. By constant improvement, I'm not talking about just putting out fires. Deming was fond of the illustration of being in a hotel when you hear someone yell 'fire!' What do you do? You run to the alarm and call the fire department. But extinguishing the fire does not improve the hotel."

Beth nodded and mumbled, "Putting out fires is different from quality improvement."

"Whew," Gary observed, "that means a lot of the stuff we do each week is not really getting us where we want to go."

"You have to put out fires," Jeff suggested. "However, when you think about quality on the front end and strive regularly to incorporate improvement methods, you're far less likely to have a lot of fires to extinguish."

"We're talking about being proactive versus reactive," Beth said.

"Excellent. Let's keep going," Jeff suggested. He pushed another key on the laptop and advanced to the next slide on Principle Six.

Principle Six:
Invest the time and money to teach, train and retrain people to develop their skills and to implement quality ministry methods.

"That's my hot button," Beth said enthusiastically. "Churches seem so quick to put people into ministry roles with little or no training, and then we wonder why people aren't more effective."

"I'd have to agree with you," Jeff admitted. "Corporate America spends billions of dollars in workshops, seminars and training sessions for its employees. My observation in the church realm is that we're significantly undertrained."

Gary asked, "Why? I'm not disagreeing with you. I just can't figure out why we do so poorly in this area."

"I'm not sure," Jeff responded. "I think it goes back to the idea of lowering the bar so that we can make it easy for people to get involved. Sometimes we make it too easy. The result is ineffective people who are poorly trained and, therefore, unhappy in their roles. Not only does service suffer, producing dissatisfied customers, but turnover is high as well. At Majesty Suites, we require all our staff to go through periodic training."

"Right," Gary countered, "but the majority of our staff at Family Church are volunteers. As an employer who pays wages, you can require your people to go through training. We have to be more sensitive to people's schedules and family time, and making too many requirements will diminish their participation."

"You're right to a degree," Jeff responded. "Yet why not include training as part of all your ministry agreements? That way, when people see what they are getting into, you can be up front with the requirements. We may lose a few people who don't see the need or can't make the time, but if we lovingly make it a standard expectation, new people will rise to the vision."

Gary questioned, "But what if we invest the time and money in training only to have them move? Don't we lose our investment?"

"If more churches trained effectively, everyone would benefit when parishioners move. It's better to train people and lose them than not train them and keep them," Jeff explained.

Beth nodded in agreement. "I think people will respond well if we raise the bar to include training. I think it would be so neat if Family Church could become a place in our community where corporations could send employees to our leadership training sessions."

Jeff hit a key and brought up Principle Seven.

Principle Seven:
The leader's job is to buy into the concept for quality concern, cast the vision and never delegate the core value.

"More than any single point, this is the key to becoming a five-star church or hotel," said Jeff. "It's got to start with your leaders."

"Whoopee," Gary cheered. "That's my hot button."

Jeff smiled. "The staff and ministry directors must be servants to everyone else to help them find a place of effectiveness. There is no such thing as wrong people, just wrong positions. A part of quality concern is helping people find their places of effectiveness. That is the responsibility of leaders."

"I know," Gary admitted. "Excellence must become a part of our fabric. It starts with me and then trickles to our ministry leaders, and only then becomes a part of our church. I can cast the vision via messages, board meetings, newsletters and staff gatherings. You don't have to convince me of this point."

The three friends paused momentarily, exchanged glances and then proceeded to jot notes and discuss in greater detail the seven principles Jeff had outlined. After an hour of rigorous deliberation, Beth suggested, "Let's take a break. I'm starting to get overloaded."

"Good idea," Jeff agreed. "Let me run up to my office to field a couple of calls, and then I'll return to go over the final seven of Deming's 14 points."

"Thanks," Gary said.

The quality-improvement process is progressive.
A church doesn't go from "terrible" to "wonderful"
in a single week! Improving quality requires
an overall culture change.

— S T A N   T O L E R

THE GIST OF IT...
WHY WE DO WHAT WE DO AND THE WAY WE DO IT

Getting a grasp of the fundamental principles is important for implementing any new practice. To start off working on action before understanding concepts is a lot like giving a person a toolbox and turning him loose to fix a car. Tools are great, but a course in auto mechanics will help him know how to use the tools.

In Exodus 20, God gave the people of Israel 10 specific standards. In subsequent chapters and the book of Leviticus, He helped them know how to implement these standards in everyday life. Paul spends the first part of Romans explaining the basics of Christianity. The latter part has to do with living out our faith.

That is why understanding the basics of quality and the pursuit of excellence is fundamental to incorporating these principles into our ministries. Deming has provided a proven structure for understanding the process. Grasping the basics allows us to later discuss how we can put these into practice on a week-to-week basis. If we do not take the time to understand the fundamentals, we will feel awkward, be frustrated and likely give up on the project. Many of us have experienced programs that we blamed as ineffective, just because we did not know how to use them. How many people reject Christianity, not on the basis of having tried it and found it lacking, but because they lacked trying it?

Let's review the first seven principles in the context of a local church.

Principle One:
We want to be the best we can be, reach our potential, serve people better and glorify God. To do this, we must be intentional and perpetual.

Taking time out intentionally to implement a system for constant quality analysis and improvement rarely happens in organizations in general, let alone faith communities. After all, we're nonprofit, voluntary and grace oriented. Unfortunately, these are often used to excuse our lack of attention to detail instead of motivating us to pursue excellence with more gusto than our corporate counterparts. Profit and survival should not be the primary motivators to pursue quality.

For some churches, it may take the threat of decline and closure to move them. For others of us, the proactive desire to grow and be our best for God will hopefully activate us to change. If we cannot clearly communicate our methods for quality improvement, the chances are that nothing will be done because concern for quality is nearly always a conscious, intentional pursuit.

Quality has to be caused, not controlled.
— PHILIP CROSBY

Principle Two:
Let's practice what we preach and put thorns in our laurels.

Talk, talk, talk. It's easy. It's cheap. It sometimes fools us into thinking we've done what we talk about. It keeps us busy, so busy that we have no time to implement what we've discussed. After all is said and done, more is said than done. That's what James wrote when he said, "Be doers of the word, and not hearers only" (Jas. 1:22, *NKJV*).

The inherent danger of sermons and Bible studies is the presumption that what we hear, we know. The New Testament uses two primary words for "know." One refers to knowing intellectually, cognitively (Greek: *oida*). The other has to do with knowing something by experience (Greek: *ghosko*). Ancient cultures were big on experience. The rise of information and education in recent years tempts us to confuse knowing with doing.

Can we point to how we will implement this new concern for quality? Just as we are to "work out our salvation" (see Phil. 2:12), how are we going to implement this quest for perpetual improvement?

Addressing these kinds of questions moves us forward toward adopting and practicing a ministry improvement plan.

Principle Three:
Everyone on the ministry team is involved in analyzing what we do, how we do it and how we can do it better to serve people best.

Like the blindfolded men trying to describe an elephant, varying perspectives provide different looks at ministry. That is why we consistently need to seek ideas and feedback from ministry people at all levels.

Personal ownership may be the answer to great customer service. When people from the ground up have the opportunity to give their ideas and implement them, they will develop a sense that this ministry is theirs. The commitment grows! The excitement of perpetual improvement and participation increases. We become owners versus renters in our thinking.

> **I** Initiate respectful accountability.
> **N** Never confuse inspection with expectation.
> **S** Select what you expect.
> **P** Performance must be measurable.
> **E** Excellence demands it.
> **C** Celebrate the victories.
> **T** Take time to follow up.
>
> —Alan Nelson

Principle Four:
Who are the best people for the ministry tasks, and what are the best resources we can afford?

Good stewardship and being cheap are different concepts. Like it or not, times have changed. People are more quality conscious than ever. Their preference is for programs that look rehearsed and printing that appears professional, to name a few. Catering to their needs and concerns have all become a part of our cultural expectations.

The church, perhaps more than any other organization, needs to care about how and where we spend our limited dollars. The temptation is to find the cheapest provider, the least expensive furnishings, the lowest bidder for service—thinking this is good stewardship!

The best way to use God's money is as the old saying goes, "The most bang for the buck." What will help us get further down the road? Sometimes, the cheapest way to go is the *worst* stewardship. We turn people off with less-than-professional publicity, lousy sound or crummy carpeting, and we end up losing people and dollars instead of attracting people and dollars.

Besides purchasing resources and services, we need to consider this concept in the context of hiring staff and employing the laity in ministry roles. The Bible never requires those who work professionally in the church realm to take the vow of poverty. Many congregations treat their pastors and staff as second-rate citizens by confining them financially, leaving them at retirement with nothing to retire on.

Many perceive stewardship as getting the most ministry we can from paying the least possible for staff. Then they wonder why more than 85 percent of churches are not growing and the average pastoral tenure is three to four years and staff is half that. Prioritizing good pay for good talent and hard work goes a long way in attracting and keeping quality people. Although money is not to be a primary motive for ministry, we cannot avoid dealing with the matter in the high-cost culture of America. A pastor must be a good steward for his spouse and family, which means looking intently at the financial package before taking a ministry position, in addition to considering the "opportunities."

Principle Five:
We need to discuss the Q (quality) factor when we plan a project, after an event and in our scheduled staff meetings.

"How did it go?" conversations should follow every significant ministry event or periodic meeting. This often seems anticlimactic because we tend to be future oriented and don't enjoy rehashing past experiences. We learn the most, however, by reviewing our performance soon after the experience. If we wait too long, our memories and perspectives fail us.

After a special event such as a children's program, youth camp, concert or church picnic, the planning staff should schedule a debriefing meeting to celebrate what went well and also record what could be done better the next time around. Without this information, we tend to repeat our performance. Practice does not make perfect; it makes permanent.

Notice the little things; send thank-you notes, flowers or gift certificates. Never be cheap in giving thanks; it's theologically and organizationally sound. By celebrating big and small improvements, we avoid the reputation of being harsh taskmasters who are never satisfied and overly critical. It is amazing how much work gets done when you recognize the "good jobs."

Principle Six:
Invest the time and money to teach, train and retrain
people to develop their skills and to implement quality
ministry methods.

If there is any single area where churches neglect to take their ministry seriously, it is in the area of training. Given the rise of the lay movement and the emergence of user-friendly technology, the need and ability to train have never been greater. A significant amount of the church budget should go back into developing people. The greatest asset of any congregation is its people, and training enhances that asset.

Although the context of this principle has to do specifically with quality-improvement training, ministry development will significantly improve the quality of your church. Just because a person has an interest or passion in any area does not qualify him or her to provide quality ministry.

Would you take a 16-year-old employee and turn him loose at the sales counter just because he was zealous? Not if you want to be successful. First, you would need to train him. In the same manner, just because a person has experience in the area of ministry, either from another church or your congregation, does not mean he or she will be equipped to provide quality ministry in a new setting.

When the benchmarks are raised and the standards are changed, retraining is required.

There is no single form for training. It varies according to types of ministry, budget constraints, local resources available, conferences and tools on the market. The key is that every ministry develops an initial orientation training before "certifying" a person for the ministry role, and then to have a written plan for continuing education. Most professions do this normally. Therefore, many people should be used to it.

Although some might balk at having to give up more time for training, most people will appreciate the extra effort to raise their potential (as long as the training is practical and well done). Many of them will pay some or all of their expenses to gain this preparation. The key for the ministry directors is to prequalify the training and make it a valuable investment of time. People are more concerned about wasting time than money these days. Make the maximum use of time in any training effort.

> *Disturb us, O Lord disturb us,*
> *O Lord, when we are too well pleased with ourselves;*
> *When our dreams come true only because*
> *we have dreamed too little.*
> *When we arrive safely only because*
> *we sailed too close to the shore,*
> *When with the abundance of things*
> *we are losing our thirst for more of God;*
> *When in loving time, we have ceased to dream of eternity,*
> *When in our desire to build on this earth*
> *we have lost our vision of a new heaven.*
> *—Anonymous*

The following are five terrific reasons to develop your staff into professional ministers, paid or other:

1. **Trained staff members are more effective.** Never assume that a minister understands the principle or ministry, unless you have seen him in action. We make far too many assumptions in the church. Aptitudes, gifts and talents are merely potentials unless effectively developed. Our goal is fruitfulness, to maximize the potential in people to help them be more productive.

2. **Trained staff members are more fulfilled.** Effective people tend to be more fulfilled. When we see lives changed, we feel fulfilled. Ineffectiveness eats away at our confidence and satisfaction. There are no theological reasons to believe that ministry has to be unfulfilling for it to be spiritual. We can both serve others and feel gratified in the same process.

3. **Trained staff members are less transient.** Ministry turnover is a perpetual problem, whether paid or voluntary. An intangible paycheck we can give people is helping them find a place of ministry where they are both effective and fulfilled. People quit high-paying positions for lack of these two qualities. Training helps people stay on the cutting edge and improve their skills, which makes them better committed. We often test the dedication of people by asking them to do tasks for which they have been inadequately trained.

4. **Trained staff members attract quality associates and members.** When we improve the effectiveness of our ministry, we tend to draw more people who want to receive what we have to offer. Too often, we set the bar too low, and the higher-achievement people are not attracted to participate. When we raise the standards for participating in a ministry, which includes training, we are apt to attract others who are quality oriented. We all want to be associated with a winning team.

5. Trained staff members raise the quality quotient.
Just as a gallon of ice lowers the average temperature of
a bucket of water, so does the quality of our ministers
raise or lower the average ministry of our church. When
you improve the effectiveness of a program or department through training, the entire church is enhanced.
When every subministry in the church has training for
quality improvement, the entire church feels the benefit.
It's easy to overlook things incrementally, but the sum
total goes up. When training enhances one ministry,
this tends to motivate other ministries to join them in
self-improvement.

> *If a man is called to be a street sweeper,*
> *he should sweep streets even as*
> *Michelangelo painted,*
> *or Beethoven composed music,*
> *or Shakespeare wrote poetry.*
> *He should sweep streets so well that all the hosts of heaven and*
> *earth will pause to say, here lived a great street sweeper*
> *who did his job well.*
> *—Martin Luther King, Jr.*

Principle Seven:
**The leader's job is to buy into the concept for quality
concern, cast the vision and never delegate the core
value.**

> *The bigger we get...the smaller we have to think.*
> *Customers still walk in one at a time.*
>
> — S A M   W A L T O N

Leadership isn't everything, as some leadership gurus would have you believe. Nevertheless, leading is the most important single element for any significant organizational change. If the leaders in a church do not have the vision for quality improvement and make it a part of their ongoing agenda, it's not going to happen. Something as thorough and permeating as a continual quality-improvement mind-set cannot be delegated.

You can delegate the accountability and strategic development phases, but the vision and constant verbalization of the need for quality concern must be a job for leaders. It starts at the top. The official and unofficial influencers in your congregation will need to help make it happen. Budgets and time resources allocated to empower and train leaders are factors in expressing quality improvement as a core value.

The role of leadership in conjunction with this principle is twofold: First, initiating a quality-improvement system is a proactive task for leaders. Most of the laity are so consumed with reactive tasks that they're not likely to jump aboard another all-encompassing plan without leaders in the saddle. Second, leaders have the responsibility of maintaining quality improvement as a core value to be continually effective.

QUESTIONS AND ANSWERS

Q. Of these seven principles, which is the most important?

Alan: Like Pastor Gary said in the narrative section, leadership is my hot button. It's the core of the Southwest Center for Leadership I direct, and the books and articles I help produce on the subject. I'd like to say this very bluntly: If there are people reading this book who are not leaders, a quality-improvement strategy WILL NOT happen unless the formal and informal leaders get on board.

There are few absolutes in life, but this is one that comes close to it. You may want it, desire it, hope for it and even think you can pull it off without the help of leadership, but my experience tells me you are bordering on delusion to think it.

The reason leaders need to buy into this plan before it happens is perhaps even more important in the church. The reason is that we have less leverage to get people to respond because we are often working with people's leftover time and energy. That is not to imply our people are not committed and motivated; but if we are to "add" another dimension to our already hectic ministry life, we must cast the vision for it.

Why do we need it? What will be the benefit of it? Answering these questions is the job of the leaders. It has to make sense for leaders directing and participating in ministries to raise the bar on their planning, execution and analysis of ministry before they will naturally expend the extra time and energy. Vision is about a preferred future. The job of the leader is to help participants visualize the possibilities within our grasp of pursuing constant improvement.

The number-one job of the pastor and leadership team is to clearly communicate the big picture—why we want to change or enhance what we have been doing. If people buy into the idea, then the leader has done his or her job. If people resist the change, and the intentional pursuit of quality improvement is never realized, chances are high the leader has failed in adequately casting the vision.

Stan: I fully agree! The first step for me at my church was to establish a leadership-training program. The church needs trained leaders who understand the need for quality in ministry. The leaders must cast a vision for a quality-focused environment. Having the added ingredient of church members who want to see quality ministry taking place...you're on the road to success.

> *We don't know who we are until*
> *we see what we can do.*
> —DERRIC JOHNSON

Q. How do I get everyone on board to buy into this new idea among all their other ideas?

Stan: Start with meetings with your key leaders and move to the "heart and soul" members of the church. Progressively win them over in terms of vision and planning. When key leaders buy into your plan of action, everyone else should follow.

Never forget that little things count. A thing cannot be too small to deserve attention. Consider these examples:

- Sir Isaac Newton studied a child's soap bubble, leading to his most important optical discoveries.
- The art of printing was suggested by a man cutting letters in the bark of a tree.
- Charles Goodyear neglected his skillet until it was red-hot and this guided him to manufacture vulcanized rubber.
- The web of a spider suggested to Captain Brown the idea of a suspension bridge.
- Watching a spider weave its web gave Robert Bruce the courage to try again.
- Henry Ford's idea about a perfect watch plant gave him the plan for his giant motor industry.
- J. L. Kraft's idea to put cheese into a sanitary package was the start of his enormous business.

Teach your key leaders to do the little things exceptionally well. The following is a series of key words to guide leaders in gaining support for a quality-improvement plan:

Listen	Create	Implement
Resource	Refine	Lead

We are what we repeatedly do.
Excellence, then, is not an act but a habit.

— ELMER TOWNS

Alan: The question is who the "I" is. If it is the pastor, then depending on your church structure, gather the formal and informal (official and unofficial) influencers in the church, especially the ministry directors, whether they are paid or volunteer staff. These are the people who will be implementing or blocking the implementation of a quality-improvement plan at a grassroots level. Everyone needs to know you as pastor; and the elder board or equivalent are going to promote, support and hold accountable the rest of the team.

Q. How in the world am I going to find the time to plan and implement a quality-improvement "program" into our already hectic ministry schedule?

Alan: You won't find it; you'll have to create it. Stephen Covey teaches us a lot about time and priorities. He uses a two-by-two matrix, comparing things that are important and urgent, important and not urgent, unimportant and urgent, and unimportant and not urgent. Investing the time to effectively plan and implement a quality-improvement plan is a quadrant-two item, meaning it is important, but not urgent.

Unfortunately, quadrant-two items are the most likely to get overlooked. We tend to be consumed with things that are important and urgent, such as writing sermons, and unimportant and urgent, such as opening mail, straightening desks and other time-consuming activities. You will eventually find that once the vision is cast and the system is running, you will have fewer fires to put out because proper planning went in on the front end. But to get going will require sacrificial time and energy.

Being in a new, fast-growing church, we are consumed with initiating numerous activities—common in an entrepreneurial setting. Our program staff and our ministry leadership team meets weekly; the true church staff consisting of paid and unpaid ministry directors meets bimonthly. We are using these meetings to develop the infrastructure for various core values training, in addition to fire-quenching items such as adding another worship service, etc.

I would not commit less than six months to making this a front-burner item in such leadership meetings. If it is to take place, I'd recommend another six months of discussing it regularly as a back-burner constant. Some congregations may need more time, such as one to three years to implement a quality-improvement plan. I can't imagine anyone doing it in a shorter amount of time, if it is to be thorough. A token lesson or two on quality ministry will have very little effect.

Stan: You're right on track! It takes a long time to achieve what we're talking about. I think the process works in this manner:

1. Understanding—what is necessary in church ministry.
2. Commitment—never underestimating the importance of dedication.
3. Strategy—implementing a plan that works.
4. Refinement—tracking and improving along the way.
5. Communication—regularly informing the church family.
6. Perseverance—the "grit" and "determination" to build a quality ministry.

Q. How do we get beyond the idea that Deming's concepts and a quality focus are just corporate, worldly philosophies?

Stan: Great question! First and foremost, we must lift up biblical models of leadership styles and then connect them to the marketplace. Next, we should share biblical examples of building campaigns in the Old Testament. Talk about doing things right. Examples abound everywhere of the finest materials being used for the house of worship.

Alan: Deming's ideas have been applied to a broad range of organizations extending from factories to service organizations. The Church is primarily a service organization because it manufactures few tangible products. Our service is a pretty important one—linking people with God. That is why a shoot-from-the-hip approach to ministry is less than what God seeks and deserves.

D. L. Moody was once criticized for his evangelism technique. Moody responded, "I'm not too fond of it either. Tell me yours." The critic admitted he didn't have one. Moody said, "I like mine better." If you can improve on Deming's ideas, go for it. Once you effectively implement Deming's ideas, improve them and help others do the same. The point is to think through the ideas for developing a deep, consistent plan for ministry improvement.

Q. We're doing okay the way we are. Why do we need to implement anything new like this?

Alan: It's your choice. No one is going to stand up in church on Sunday and yell, "Can't we do better?" Probably no first-time guest will ever call or write to give you ideas about why they will not be back. But in a consumer-oriented, post-Christian culture in which most of us find ourselves, a lack of concerted effort to implement continual improvement in our various ministry areas will cause us to plateau, if not decline.

Nearly every other organization that is growing is seeking quality improvement. Why do we think the Church is any different?

Some might say, "Well, we do pretty well the way we are, striving to improve as we go." That may be true. But a hit-and-miss approach involving no strategic plan for quality improvement is apt to be more miss than hit. Like we said before, most of us are so consumed with just doing what we need to do that if there is not a core-value change, we will more than likely overlook significant, regular improvement. The temptation to perpetuate yesterday's programs as they are is powerful.

Stan: How true! I have just led Trinity Church through a diagnostic period. Ultimately, we concluded that after 63 years of "customer" service to the community, we were doing some things exceedingly well. On the other hand, we also listened to church members who told us about the lack of ministries to families, inadequate parking and the needs of children and more educational space. What an eye-opener. If the Church doesn't become prayerfully diagnostic, we will fail in our efforts to reach an unchurched culture.

THE DOERS SECTION

- Discuss the first seven principles of a quality-improvement plan.
- Why must quality improvement be intentional instead of assuming we are already doing well?
- In what ways do we already express our concern for quality?
- What would it take for us to implement a quality-improvement plan?
- How can we obtain feedback from the vital leaders of each church ministry?
- Who are the best people for the ministry tasks?
- What are the best resources we can afford?
- What method will we use to check the quality of our equipment and resources that we are currently using in the various ministries?
- What can we do to make sure we are getting the right people for the positions versus the "warm body" syndrome?
- Discuss the Q (quality) factor as you plan a project in your scheduled staff meetings.
- How can we discuss quality elements during our regular ministry meetings?
- What do we need to do to make sure we talk about how things went after an event or program?
- How much do we currently spend to train our staff—paid and volunteer?
- How could we improve the training of our staff regarding quality improvement and ministry skills in general?

- Discuss: Do you agree or disagree with the emphasis placed on leadership for making sure a quality-improvement plan takes place in your church?
- Is leadership on board regarding such a plan? If so, what role will the leaders play in keeping this on the front burner until it becomes a part of our church fabric?

There is little difference in people,
but that little difference makes the big difference.
The little difference is attitude.

— W. CLEMENT STONE

My Utmost for His Highest

★ ★ ★ ★ ★

Efficiency is getting the job done right.
Effectiveness is getting the right job done.
Excellence is getting the right job done well.

— ZIG ZIGLAR

Jeff entered the meeting room and asked, "All right, have we had enough of a break?"

"I'm game," Gary responded. "My head is swirling with ways we can implement these ideas at Family Church, but let's keep moving."

"This can be overwhelming, but the goal is to see the big picture first," Jeff commented.

"Isn't it kind of like when Moses got the Ten Commandments?" Beth asked. "The basic ten were pretty simple, but the children of Israel spent a long time figuring out how the Law would transform the way they developed their nation."

"Good point, Beth," said Gary. "You know, I have to remember that our goal is to help Family Church serve Christ and others with excellence. Nothing but the best."

"My Utmost for His Highest," Beth replied. "That was a pretty catchy title of an Oswald Chambers book, but the idea is ageless."

"Okay," Jeff said, "let's wrap up the last half of the 14 principles for a quality ministry-improvement plan." He flipped on the video projector and advanced the computer to the next slide.

Principle Eight:
Provide a safe, secure environment to share ideas.

"In other words, we're to drive out fear," Jeff explained. "The word 'secure' is from the Latin words *se*, meaning without, and *cure*, meaning fear. If we are to positively critique what we're doing and help people participate in the process, we have to make sure they feel secure."

"That's contrary to human nature," Beth pointed out. "Our first response when we hear that something is wrong with our ministry is to defend it."

"I resemble that remark," Gary said with a smile. "My wife knows never to critique my message, at least not right after a service." The three friends laughed.

Jeff's eyes brightened as he continued his explanation. "But we've got to have the freedom to bring up ideas for change. New ideas are like newborns. They need to be nurtured and treated delicately. The tendency is to think that the way we've always done it is fine, so let's not rock the boat. Unfortunately, if we consider idea givers as troublemakers, we'll completely close the creative process that will make us better."

Gary asked, "How do we make it safe to share ideas and try new things?"

"Part of it goes back to training," Jeff answered, "especially among the ministry leaders. They have to feel secure enough to let anyone share an idea without taking it personally. Then they have to make sure that new ideas and the people who bring them up feel accepted and affirmed."

Beth responded, "Hey, if the Church can't provide that, who can?"

"True," Jeff added. "Unfortunately, the Church is made up of people who come to God—baggage and all. A part of a continual quality-improvement plan means that we regularly brainstorm on how we could do better, so that new ideas are plentiful. Some ideas are implemented; many are passed up for better ones. Yet all ideas and idea givers find a nonthreatening, welcome environment."

"I don't disagree with you," Gary suggested, "but how do you deal with chronic complainers if you provide too much room for critique and idea sharing?"

Beth rolled her eyes and asked, "Yes, what can you do?"

"At first," Jeff responded, "that can be a problem, as complainers see this as a chance to pass on their pessimism. But through proper training and in your case, preaching, you can distinguish between a positive critique and a complaining spirit. Of course, Paul tells us in Philippians to do everything without complaining and arguing."

"I agree," Gary affirmed. "I've seen a lot more congregations split over worship and ministry styles than I have on theological differences."

"The teaching idea on constructive versus destructive sharing is good," Beth added. "We need to develop that further as a discipleship issue."

Gary and Beth nodded in agreement as they scribbled down a flurry of notes. The next principle was flashed on the screen.

Principle Nine:
Build a team mind-set to avoid departmental barriers.

Jeff took a run at explaining its meaning. "The goal is to get us thinking and acting like a single team instead of many little teams," he said. "As a church grows, it tends to become departmentalized. The youth ministry does its thing. The worship team does its thing. The children's ministry does its thing. The more we think of our own little ministry domains, the less prone we are to see the big picture and help each other."

Beth asked, "What about smaller congregations?"

"Individualistic thinking takes place at all levels and sizes of organizations," Jeff explained. "Large congregations must be more intentional in creating teamwork, but even small churches cannot assume that everyone is working together. There must be some periodic gathering place where people can communicate, share ideas, and even critique each other's ministries and programs. Some of the best insights are gained through other people's perspectives."

Gary asked, "It's pretty easy to get tunnel vision, isn't it?"

"Yes, and it's because of our motivation to take care of our own limited area of work or ministry," Jeff answered.

"How do you get individual ministry leaders to take the extra time to gather as a team when they are already donating time in their individual ministries?" Beth asked. "And how do you help them see the importance of team building? Sometimes we've tried this, and the staff feel it is a waste of their time, when they could be working on their specific ministry needs."

"I hear your frustration," Jeff said. "To help your people see the need to invest the time and energy will require education and vision casting. Again, this will be different from what you've done in the past. Whether you promote it as a new idea to implement or as a step for bettering your church by getting valuable input, your job as a leader is to sell the value in getting together. However, whenever you raise the benchmark with new expectations, you also have to give people the freedom to decline."

"We may lose ministry leaders with this new plan," Beth commented.

"You may," Jeff agreed, "but nevertheless, the other issue here is in structuring these team meetings so that they do not waste people's time. Help them see the benefits of everyone brainstorming about our children's ministry. The youth, worship and mission leaders must not feel you're wasting their time even though they may not be directly involved in children's ministry. If you help ministry leaders see the importance of getting the big picture and make

Family Church the beneficiary of their individual input, quality ideas will emerge."

"I like that," interjected Gary. "That comes down to the leader and the leadership team."

"You've got it," Jeff said, who advanced the next principle to the screen.

Principle Ten:
Eliminate slogans and short-term goals.

"Wait a second," Gary interrupted. "You're tampering with years of tradition here."

A smile creased Jeff's lips. He replied, "We're not talking about a new building-fund slogan or outreach campaign titles. We want to avoid the typical short-term thinking that provides only temporary motivation or improvement."

"In other words, quality improvement is long term, ongoing," Beth said.

"Right," Jeff replied. "At least we don't want to give the impression that we've discovered some program that will fix things. People can be cynical with all the fads and hype these days, so slogans and short-term goals actually weaken our focus on deeper objectives of excellence."

"That makes sense," Gary said. "This will help me know how to develop this idea to avoid making it seem like a program or seasonal fad."

Jeff advanced to the next slide.

Principle Eleven:
Avoid numerical goals.

"Don't play the numbers game," Jeff counseled. "I used to think that only businesses focused on numbers. Yet the more I hang around pastors and church leaders, the more I realize we're not alone."

"You ought to hear the numbers dropping that goes on in ministerial circles," Gary said.

"It's not just pastors though," Beth added. "The local church grapevine keeps track of which congregations are growing and which ones are losing members."

"We're not just talking about money or worship service attendance," Jeff said. "Figures can fool you. They are not unimportant, but they should not be our main goal. When quality service becomes the main thing, growth usually follows. As John 15 says, if you *abide* in Christ, you will bear fruit. Therefore, our goal is not to bear fruit, but to abide, because if we abide, we will be fruitful."

"Seems like I heard that somewhere recently," Gary laughed.

"I just wanted to know if you listened to your own sermons," Jeff said with an impish grin.

"Like you said," Beth interjected, "you never go out to an orchard and hear trees groaning to make an apple. Fruit grows naturally if the trees are watered and nurtured."

"Good point," Jeff said. "Let's see how it relates to Principle Twelve."

Principle Twelve:
Give people ownership.

Gary and Beth nodded in agreement as Jeff elaborated, "Tear down barriers that prevent the people from developing a healthy pride in what they do. Provide a freedom to do what it takes to add their personal touch. Obviously, there are limitations that fit within the church as a whole, but if people don't feel the ministry is theirs, they will usually add little to its improvement."

"Aren't we talking about empowerment?" Beth suggested.

"Yes, empowerment," Jeff agreed. "But true empowerment means an unleashing of influence and resources, not just verbal permission. It goes back to the Old and New Testament passages that talk about all of God's people being 'a royal priesthood, a holy nation,' and that we each have a unique function in the Body of Christ."

Gary asked, "So how do you prevent rogue members from taking their newfound freedom to reckless arenas of ministry?"

"Whew, nice wording," Beth said. "Rogue members, eh?"

"Well…"

Jeff jumped in. "It comes down to leadership development and proper vision casting. Within reason, the bottom line is, some entrepreneurial ministers will be the best thing for a church to keep it changing, growing and on the cutting edge. The key again is not so much what, but with what spirit. When people have the right attitude and exhibit teamwork, they are usually safe. When they never cross the line and remain aloof, apathetic and cynical, do they really add to the team?"

"I get it," Gary exclaimed.

"Good," Jeff continued. "Here's Principle Thirteen."

Principle Thirteen:
Vigorously educate people.

"Didn't we have that one before?" Beth inquired, flipping back over her note sheets. "Here it is. Principle Six says, 'Invest the time and money to teach, train and retrain people to develop their skills and to implement quality ministry methods.'"

"They are definitely related," responded Jeff, "but different enough to warrant separate principles. Point six has to do with training, which emphasizes behavior and skills. Principle Thirteen is about continuous education, which has more to do with big-picture ideas and understanding them."

"Can you give us an example of the two?"

"Sure, Beth," Jeff replied. "For example, ministry training may have to do with how we prepare our nursery staff to work with our security-check system or how to change diapers using sterile procedures and proper handling of infants. However, education might include a class on infant psychology or a trip to a local church's nursery to observe how it operates. Training focuses on application—what we do. Education emphasizes the bigger picture—what we can learn about the field."

"I suppose they cross over with each other," Beth suggested.

"Beth, they do," Jeff agreed. "Yet training without education tends to turn us toward becoming robots who may be programmed to perform certain skills, but are not apt to improve the skills because we've run across new ideas. Education keeps us fresh mentally and exposes us to a wider range of information that can help us improve our quality. Continuing education is the key to staying on the cutting edge in a culture that is changing constantly. Investing in conferences, classes, periodicals, cassettes and videos keeps our people sharp."

Jeff inquired, "Are you ready for our last principle?" When he saw the nodding heads, he advanced the computer presentation.

Principle Fourteen:
Head into action.

"At the beginning," Jeff explained, "we talked about adopting the idea of a continual quality-improvement plan, but now we're talking about implementing it."

"This is the 'what's next' step," Gary concluded.

"Right. We're back to the 'practice what you preach' concept."

"Okay," Gary asked, "so what is next for us at Family Church?"

Jeff elaborated, "We need to sit down, the three of us or more, to talk about how we might develop a big-picture view of how we'll begin to incorporate these principles into Family Church, and then follow that action plan."

"Why don't we each draft some ideas," Gary asked, "and then come back to initiate an action plan?"

"Great idea, Jeff," Beth said. "I can see how a quality-improvement plan can transform everything we do, making our ministry more effective and exciting. I'm a bit overwhelmed right now, but excited."

"Me too," Gary agreed. "I think my biggest concern is that we don't try to do too much at the beginning."

The three friends talked more about the possibilities of helping Family Church pursue excellence intentionally and passionately. Then they left to develop an action plan.

THE GIST OF IT...
WHY WE DO WHAT WE DO AND THE WAY WE DO IT

The tendency to forget why we're doing what we're doing is strong, especially when you're considering a new way of approaching ministry. Here's a good checklist to follow:

Principle Eight:
Provide a safe, secure environment to share ideas.

Because churches often function more like family than corporate counterparts, we behave differently in various situations. Sometimes we squabble more and yet stay on board because, well, that's what families do. At other times, we settle for less because family members tend to see and accept us the way we are.

We hopefully can turn our loving, accepting culture into a wholesome environment of self-improvement and ministry growth. By teaching people about the quality-improvement plan, we give permission to openly discuss concerns and any ideas without the threat of retaliation or rejection.

Part of the training should involve giving leaders and people ideas about how to communicate a suggestion and how to avoid hurting feelings. When this fails to happen, openness shuts down and participants nod obligingly to the leader's ideas, holding their own ideas to themselves or expressing their suggestions through the coffee-table grapevine. Strive to not only make it okay to share ideas, but also to affirm and reward suggestions. Model it from the top!

Principle Nine:
Build a team mind-set to avoid departmental barriers.

The strength of focusing on a single ministry area becomes a weakness when we seek to work as a team. The reason is that it is difficult to maintain both the small picture and the big picture at the same time. The job of the pastor and board is to continually cast the big vision and bring together ministry directors for the purpose of hearing each other and building teamwork.

When we see ourselves as "us," we are less likely to view other ministries as "them." Although we may never admit this openly, most churches and organizations tend toward compartmentalization. We compete over budgets, resources, space, workers—even participants.

Gathering ministry leaders periodically to build relationships and help each other listen to one another is an important part of breaking down departmental walls. Because so many ties exist between the various subministries of a congregation, working together is important.

Principle Ten:
Eliminate slogans and short-term goals.

Churches are notorious for cute slogans and catchy clichés. As a whole, nothing is wrong with this, but when it comes to developing a continual quality-improvement system, short-term slogans tend to undercut your effectiveness.

The main reason is that the task is significant. Slogans wear off quickly. The phrase may stick, but the meaning behind it loses punch. We can easily fool ourselves into believing we really are doing something significant regarding improvement just because we see banners and quality logos plastered around the facility or printed in the church mailings.

Churches must design a strategic plan of action to achieve their own unique quality-improvement system. Again, for this idea to bear fruit, it needs to become a part of ongoing ministry planning.

Principle Eleven:
Avoid numerical goals.

Most churches will significantly need to increase the use of numbers, which tend to provide feedback where improvement is and is not needed. Whether it is a ministry survey from past, present or potential participants, or a line chart looking at attendance and offerings, we want to avoid overly subjective opinions by decision makers.

Although many businesses and corporations rely heavily on statistical data, a church does very little of this. We tend to rely almost solely on the big three: attendance, offerings and membership (for those who have membership). We will talk later about developing an array of measuring instruments that will help us validate what is going well and not going well in our ministry area.

In general, we want to avoid numerical goals in regard to quality. The reason tends to be twofold. First of all, goals can be self-defeating. If we set a goal and do not accomplish it, we can feel bad when, in fact, we may have improved the ministry.

Conversely, if we set a numeric goal and achieve it, the tendency is to think we're doing great and then let down our concern for continual quality improvement.

Principle Twelve:
Give people ownership.

This is the "trick" of any leadership objective. How can we get team members to see continual quality improvement as their goal and not something the pastor or ministry director came up with after attending some slick seminar or reading the latest book?

After the vision has been cast to develop a quality-improvement plan, the process tends to significantly enhance ministry ownership because it relies heavily on feedback and ideas, as well as implementation, from those who are active in the ministry.

This is not a top-down, canned idea. Rather, the ministry leader facilitates discussion between the workers and volunteers to generate ideas about how we can do better. The leader is not the answer source. He or she is a participant but has a responsibility to let the ideas flow without intimidation and then facilitate an action plan for employing the better ideas.

Most ministry participants believe their ideas are not valued. We assume that silence means they are happy with how things are and they have no ideas for making it better. That assumption is wrong. We need to assume that every worker and ministry user has ideas that are untapped because we fail to provide safe forums for them to express their ideas. When workers begin to express ideas that become a part of the ongoing ministry in which they are involved, ownership rises significantly.

Principle Thirteen:
Vigorously educate people.

In nearly every aspect of life, the more we know and understand the operation of things, the better we perform. Whatever the topic, education allows us to expand our thinking and raise our level of quality. When the Bible was translated into the common languages of the people following the invention of the Gutenberg press, biblical knowledge soared as the masses educated themselves by using the Scriptures.

Invest in sending your ministry leaders and workers to seminars, workshops and conferences. Pay for them to be mentored by another local leader who is demonstrating expertise in a ministry area. Subscribe to magazines. Purchase audios, videos and books to educate your people.

Don't just utilize church resources. Secular conferences, workshops and courses can often generate significant knowledge that can be easily translated into the church.

Principle Fourteen:
Head into action.

The final principle—taking action—is the most difficult. Without this step, the other thirteen are mere expenditures of time and energy. Jesus had many people who said they wanted to follow Him, but very few took action.

The rest of this book is designed to help you implement the principles we have introduced. However, talk without action is fruitless. The goal is to begin implementing small and large actions that reflect a continual quality-improvement plan. Think in terms of baby steps, not giant leaps. The journey is long, but don't let the length intimidate you.

QUESTIONS AND ANSWERS

Q. How do you avoid naysayers when you give them safety in sharing their ideas?

Alan: When you're fasting, the first day or two is the most difficult, often because your body is flushing toxins out of your system, which can result in headaches or mild nausea. When you deep-clean your house, sometimes the old homestead looks a lot worse before it gets better.

These are illustrations of what is likely to happen when you begin seeking ideas from ministry workers and ministry users. You may be inundated at first by people who have held back or never felt safe to share their ideas. A part of the quality-improvement training is helping your ministry leaders to deal with complaints and criticisms and to translate them into less personal, more constructive words.

If someone says, "I'm sick of the crummy way my child is checked in at the nursery," the response might be, "Nursery check-in is important. Specifically, what could we do to make it better?" Feedback such as this tends to open communication and allow ministry staff to find the solution without taking it personally.

Sometimes when you ask for ideas, you may get none. This is a sign that openness has not been welcomed. People have given up on the possibility of sharing a new thought so they quit thinking them. It may take some priming of the pump and repeated meetings until a flow of ideas is generated.

The goal of the ministry leader is to provide an environment in which constant quality improvement is the norm and not the exception. When this is done regularly, chronic complainers tend to dissipate. When you take the wind out of the sail of complainers by listening and thanking them for their input, you diminish their influence.

The problem is that naysayers, chronic complainers and negative people tend to share their ideas, whether they are asked or not. Therefore, you are apt to hear a disproportional number of criticisms from a few individuals. Every group has these unhealthy people who tend to verbalize from low self-esteem rather than a desire to better a church.

When you create regular opportunities to harvest ideas from others, the more positive people step forward. A proactive environment results in positive energy to handle suggestions for change and betterment, which actually seems to diminish the energy created by a complainer.

Stan: In a recent seminar I attended, an MIT professor named Peter Senge said, "When people talk, the vision grows clearer." I believe the negative and positive comments received in church vision meetings help us get to what is important. We can learn a great deal from parishioners who do not necessarily see it "our" way.

Pastors should welcome input from the negative elements of their churches as long as they are presented in a Christlike manner. Usually, unfortunate outbursts at meetings are avoided through establishing guidelines for brainstorming.

For the church to move forward and implement a vision plan, all elements of the church must move to the same page. I love the story of the man who was driving a little too fast on a wet road and slid into a ditch. A farmer came by with his horse named Duke and offered to pull the man's car out of the drainage ditch.

The farmer hitched his horse to the car and said, "Pull, Bill, pull!" His horse named Duke did not budge.

Then the farmer said, "Pull, Sadie, pull!" His horse still didn't move.

Finally the farmer cried, "Pull, Duke, pull!" The massive horse lunged forward and effortlessly pulled the car out of the ditch.

The distressed motorist, filled with gratitude, thanked the farmer and then asked, "Why did you call your horse the wrong name twice?"

"My horse is blind," explained the farmer, "and if he thought he was the only horse pulling, he would not even try!"

It takes teamwork in ministry to build a great work from God. Listen to all voices and then attempt to build a church for God's glory.

—ALAN NELSON

Q. How can you help people catch the big picture when they are involved in specific ministries for their limited available time?
Stan: I think it is a six-step process:

1. An emphasis on doing things right must flow through the various committee systems of the church.
2. Continuous information must be shared through the church leadership rank and file.
3. Strategic planning, with an emphasis on creativity, must be encouraged.
4. Values and principles of growth within a biblical context must be espoused.

5. A willingness to be flexible and change must be a current reality.
6. Training moments must reflect the heart of the leader, and the key strategies that will help the church achieve its purpose should be communicated.

Alan: Developing a continual improvement plan must be intentional, but most of it can be done alongside ongoing ministry meetings, as a part of training sessions, and in letter and newsletter communication. Maintaining this idea is easier than initiating it.

Like most people today, few of us have empty hours that need filling. We will need to elevate the vision and idea for quality improvement if our team members will make it a part of their active schedule. One of the best ways to initiate the idea is through a message series on excellence and service, followed by orientation training among leaders at a weekend retreat.

Realize this will be a long-term, ongoing process. Implement it right away in new ministries. Let existing ministries catch the idea. Some may never implement them because some people respond poorly to change, although others embrace it warmly and quickly. The main idea is to make sure the pastor and ministry leaders, paid or volunteer, are equipped and willing to participate. If the leaders don't lead it, it won't happen.

Q. How can we develop measurable standards for ministry quality?

Alan: As a pastor, I think one reason so many of us are into the basic attendance and membership numbers is because so much of what we do is intangible. Spiritual and character growth tend to be incremental, arduous processes. To validate our work, we often rely heavily on the weekly attendance counts.

At other times, we diminish the importance of these numbers to avoid appearing insignificant. The issue here, for most of us, is to significantly expand the number and diversity of ministry measures. In the appendices section at the back of this book, we offer some examples of questionnaires and surveys that can help us continually improve.

The goal is not to get bogged down, but to develop frequent feedback and analysis about what we're doing. One way to gain more ideas for improvement is to be consistent in seeking feedback. Creativity is often quite sporadic. If you do not have a regular way to harvest ideas, good ones will not be discovered because they will come when you're not taking a survey or asking for ideas. Let me list some ways to begin measuring quality ministry:

- Chart the last five years of church attendance, membership and finances.
- Chart the last two or three years of growth for various ministries, classes and events.
- Provide quarterly congregational surveys, one-half or one page in length, that seek information in a different ministry area each time.
- Provide an ongoing, user-friendly system for new ideas (it could be a suggestion box, a place in the church bulletin, or by receiving correspondence from a fax machine or through e-mail).
- Provide a recognition system for new ideas suggested and used for ministry improvement.
- Get anonymous feedback surveys from Sunday School class members (once or twice a year), small groups, seminars, special events and periodically at worship services.
- Reward newcomers with incentives for returning feedback questionnaires after their visits.

The difference between ordinary and
extraordinary is that little extra.

—JOHN MAXWELL

Stan: Someone has said, "Today's preparation determines tomorrow's achievement." My longtime mentor and friend, Ponder Gilliland, taught me nearly 20 years ago to ask three important questions in the local church. They are as follows:

1. What are we doing to attract people to our church?
2. How do we treat guests when they attend our church services?
3. What do we do once they have come and gone?

Frankly, I try to teach the church family that we must use the analogy of inviting people into our homes in order to do quality ministry.

FIVE-STAR CHURCH
QUALITY GOALS FOR TRINITY CHURCH

We will always seek to speak an encouraging word to our guests.

We will focus on our strengths and seek to improve our weaknesses.

We will strive to build quality ministry action teams.

We will be thoughtful and Christlike in every relationship.

We will cultivate physical, mental and spiritual growth.

We will treat others as we hope others will treat us.

We will ask, listen and hear—to determine the felt needs and potential of each newcomer.

We will seek the guidance of the Holy Spirit in every decision-making opportunity.

Q. What is the difference between ministry ownership and possessiveness? People who think of a ministry as "theirs" seem pretty opposed to others suggesting changes.

Stan: During the time I was pastoring the historic Nashville First Church of the Nazarene during the early 1990s, I became familiar with country music. A group named the Oak Ridge Boys had a hit song that has stuck in my mind. I can't remember the title, but the following lyrics stand out: "Nobody wants to play rhythm guitar behind Jesus, everybody wants to be the lead singer in the band!"

Wow! I think we have to build into our members an "All for the Kingdom" mentality. Essentially, we must teach our church family that everything we do is connected to Romans 15:17: "Therefore I glory in Christ Jesus in my service to God."

Alan: I think the main difference between a two-year-old and a team player is two words—"mine" versus "ours." If you really want to be spiritual and theological, we should say, "God's." Psychologists refer to it as ego involvement—the concept that the more I pour myself into a project, the more committed I am to it.

That is one of the secrets behind lay involvement and church and financial dedication. The more a person gets involved in a ministry of the church, the more likely that person will give both time and money to support the church and specific ministry. The idea of paying a professional staff member to do my ministry for me is counterproductive. Thus, you want a certain amount of ownership, and with it comes a certain amount of possessiveness. People who claim to own a ministry, but give no defense or challenge to new ideas and change, probably own less than we think.

A more tangible way to reduce possessiveness is to develop ministry agreements, which include important items such as gifts needed for the ministry, responsibility to someone, time expectations and time limit for the role. By including time limits of 6 to 12 months, you not only enlist those who might fear a long-term commitment, but you also exclude those who are tempted to believe in squatters rights and alienate others from infringing on "their" ministry.

Q. Can you please give us some examples of continuing education for various ministries?

Alan: Obvious options are seminars and workshops hosted by organizations such as the Willow Creek Association, INJOY Ministries and any one of more than a dozen teaching church conferences that usually provide general church ideas and renewal as well as specific ministry workshops. Youth Specialties and *Group* magazine host an array of youth and children's training events. More customized programs can be designed by bringing in a special speaker or expert, whether it is a growing church staffer or a consultant.

Although these workshops can provide education and training, we should not overlook equivalent resources in the secular realm. For example, a computer and high-tech trade show can provide incredible ideas for audiovisual improvement for any church and church office. Because high tech is amoral, we should consider these as tools for us to expand God's kingdom.

You can send children, youth and senior adult workers to CPR and first-aid seminars. Pay their ways to visit other thriving churches locally or across the country and offer to pay the appropriate staff member for an hour or two of personal time and idea sharing.

Stan: We live in a great day to minister! When I started out as a 17-year-old pastor (God bless those folks in Newark, Ohio!), seminars and great resources were scarce. In addition to all the organizations Alan has mentioned, we have training videotapes available through Gospel Light in Ventura, California, and Ephesians Four Ministries in Lynchburg, Virginia, not to mention a Christian bookstore in nearly every community in America.

THE DOERS SECTION

Discuss, think about and strategize about the last seven principles of a quality improvement plan.

- **Provide a safe, secure environment to share ideas.**
  What can we do to make it safe for people to share their ideas for ministry improvement? How and when can we

get ideas from workers and customers for ministry improvement?

- **Build a team mind-set to avoid departmental barriers.** What can we do to break down departmental barriers? How can we get team leaders of varying ministries to discuss quality-improvement ideas for our church as a whole and each other's ministries?
- **Eliminate slogans and short-term goals.** What can we do to promote the concept of continual quality improvement without relying on slogans and short-term goals?
- **Avoid numerical goals.** How can we gather feedback from people for ministry-improvement ideas without relying on numerical goals?
- **Give people ownership.** How can we improve ownership of those involved in various ministries? What can we do to gather ideas from workers without offending those whose ideas we do not use? How do we determine what ideas we'll try to implement?
- **Vigorously educate people.** Think of and discuss ways education could help improve the quality of ministries in our church. Brainstorm about ways to expand the education process of multiple ministries in the church.
- **Head into action.** Who should be involved in developing a strategic plan of action?

High expectations are the key to everything.

— S A M   W A L T O N

Excellence as a Process

★ ★ ★ ★ ★

Success is a journey, not destination.

— BOB RICHARDS

Jeff, Gary and Beth greeted each other as they sat down at the Majesty Suites' elegant Capers restaurant.

"This five-star church idea is so exciting," Gary remarked. "I can really see how we can become a place where people love to attend. What is tough is how we implement this. We've always tried to improve here and there, but not intentionally and certainly not systematically."

Beth picked up the conversation. "We've talked about the 14 principles, and they are wonderful. We've had some great ideas about the action plan, but they seem rather helter-skelter."

Jeff put them at ease. "You're doing a great job of thinking about the fundamentals of Family Church. I have no doubt that we'll see significant improvements, but I do need to emphasize, however, that the essence of excellence is more a process than a product."

Gary questioned, "What do you mean by that, Jeff?"

"What I mean is that most doers get excited about the action-plan concept but tend to overestimate the importance of excellence as a product. In other words, the process of a continual improvement plan is what we want to emphasize. If we prioritize the way we pursue quality, excellence will be a by-product."

Beth interjected, "Are you saying that we shouldn't become too outcome oriented at first?"

"Yes," answered Jeff. "Gary, remember when we talked about your teaching on John 15, the 'I am the vine' passage?"

"I remember the passage and our talk, but I'm not sure about the connection here."

"John 15, as you know, is where Jesus says He is the vine and we are the branches, and if we abide in Him, we will bear much fruit. Our main goal as Christians should not be to bear fruit; it should be abiding in Christ, because if we do, we will bear fruit," Jeff said.

"You know," Gary chimed in, "we've talked about this same idea in the context of ministry involvement. One of the most important reasons for Christians to utilize their spiritual gifts is that it helps them grow as they serve others. Part of that growth is learning how to work with others in ministry. It's so easy in a church to get task oriented—turning out a good worship service or organizing the Sunday School program. Unfortunately, we some-times get so task oriented that we get impatient and angry with people, fraying emotions in the process."

"See, I knew you'd get it," said Jeff. "That's the basic principle we're dealing with here. The nice thing a church has over organiza-tions like Majesty Suites or a regular business is that we agree that getting along with each other is a priority in the Christian faith. The business world doesn't have that basic advantage."

"If that's true," Beth asked, "why do for-profit organizations seem to outperform most churches when it comes to excellence?"

"Well, most businesses, like most churches, are not excellence orient-ed in the beginning," Jeff explained. "The five-star rating is not common. But I think churches in the past got away with lower standards because of that 'family-feel' and relationship orientation."

Beth added, "Of course, that doesn't even consider the fact that

God deserves our best. But how do we make sure the process is our main product?"

"Developing an excellence process will be the job of you and our ministry leaders," Jeff responded. "Leaders are caretakers of the culture. Until it becomes a natural process at Family Church, you will need to intentionally train, monitor and cultivate the process of a quality orientation. Let me give you five questions to ask that reflect excellence as a process versus just an outcome."

Gary and Beth pulled out their pens and notepads.

"Ready? The first question we need to ask is: How are we facilitating safe idea sharing? In other words, are the ministry leaders gifted or skilled in nurturing quality-improvement discussions without getting defensive and allowing conflicts to fester? Ask nearly any leader, 'Do you allow for safe idea sharing?' They should say, 'Sure.' Yet the way to see if a leader is doing a good job in that area is by looking for the practice in meeting agendas, asking team members and using a neutral, third party in surveying the team."

Jeff continued, "The second question is: Do we talk about how we're doing the process itself? Communication specialists call this 'metacommunication,' which has to do with talking about how we're communicating."

"With all due respect," Gary interrupted, "this sounds like a lot of counseling-type action. Doesn't this bog you down in short meeting times?"

"Different personality types can under use and over use this," Jeff responded. "If we don't talk from time to time about how we're communicating and facilitating idea sharing then the rest of what we do becomes kind of a joke."

Gary replied, "I can see that you need to be sensitive to the various temperaments on your ministry team. I also see your point on why we need to talk about the process itself. I've not done this well, except in obvious times of conflict or misunderstanding."

"Right," said Jeff. "Our goal is to be proactive, not just reactive. If we pave the way for healthy communication, we're far less apt to have open and hidden conflict. Anyway, let's go to the third question: Do we inspect what we expect? Remember, the best-laid plans often go unused because we never follow up to see if we're doing what we agreed to do."

Beth asked, "How do you avoid being a watchdog who is always policing people? That's a tough role to fill."

"Yes," Gary added, "and it consumes valuable time that you need for other things. It seems to me that most leaders are not gifted in the detailed follow-through that inspection often requires."

"Good points by both of you," said Jeff. "Let me take Beth's first. Accountability is different from watchdogging. Accountability is mutual and, hopefully, prearranged and negotiated so that everyone agrees on the way to implement the idea or change. When you see a discrepancy in what you agreed to do, people skills are very important to affirm what is good and remind you what was to be done.

"You can say a lot if you're smiling," Jeff continued. "Again, personalities respond differently to feedback and accountability, so you want to respond appropriately to the person. Some people like it short and direct. Others need much affirmation, while others prefer low-key feedback. One of the best reasons for coming up with measurable feedback is that it makes it difficult for a ministry leader to deny what the statistics say. You want to avoid personal, subjective opinions and rely on data from surveys and growth patterns."

"People-skills training and leader selection again," Beth opined.

"You're right," said Jeff. "Now, Gary, just because inspection needs to take place doesn't mean the leader has to do it. He or she just needs to make sure it gets done. If it is going to be a top priority, the leader should be involved, just as we discussed the need for making quality improvement a church's core value. You cannot delegate some things. The leader needs to find someone who has managerial and administrative gifts, or an assistant leader who is assigned to track the progress. You can also develop tools, such as a reporting system that requests feedback in a specific area you want to inspect."

"Paperwork?"

"No, Gary, a feedback system," Jeff responded. "Keep it brief. Do it via e-mail or by telephone. Every situation is different. Experiment with various ways of accountability, but never expect what you are not willing to inspect."

"It's almost as if you don't need to try to implement it if you're not willing to follow up and inspect it later," Beth commented.

"People are so busy that we tend to do just enough to get by," Jeff reasoned. "It's just human nature. If quality is a core value, we must prioritize it in our meetings and communication."

Beth and Gary nodded.

"All right," Jeff said, "let's continue. The fourth question to ask ourselves is: Do we specifically discuss the quality factor in planning and postmortems?"

"Hey, I do funerals," Gary joked. "Postmortems should be right down my line."

"Not to be insensitive," said Jeff, "but a postmortem is basically the same as performing an autopsy, regardless of how much life the program did or did not exude. The most overlooked quality-improvement conversations get passed up because we are so ready to get on with the next event or because we're so exhausted from the last event."

"I've got to admit, I'm not a leftovers guy," Gary commented.

Beth noted, "It is also difficult to get our volunteer staff to commit to another meeting time to discuss the postmortems."

"The task seems large now because we are cultivating a quality-improvement culture," said Jeff. "However, once that culture is established, feedback and review become natural habits."

Gary offered a puzzled look and asked, "What's the secret of making it a part of our culture?"

"Begin by putting it on the agenda," Jeff responded. "You can also send out surveys, put together a conference call, e-mail each other or just hold a stand-up meeting following the event. The key is to get it done, take notes and employ the feedback into future events and programs."

"That's a big one," Beth said. "People get discouraged if you're always talking improvement but they never see their ideas implemented."

"True," acknowledged Jeff, "if you want to motivate people, then you have to listen and implement their ideas. Certainly not all ideas have the same level of value, but if people see someone's idea used, they will want to participate with their own."

Gary cautioned, "But I have seen people with personal agendas push their ideas on an event or program at the expense of quality performance and execution."

"Yes, and this naturally brings us to the fifth and final question: How do we confront people when discrepancies arise in quality-improvement plans while celebrating small and large advancements in quality?"

Gary nodded. "Yes, Jeff, how do we find the balance between confronting a weakness in an undertaking or ministry while still being able to affirm the strengths?"

"Several years ago," Jeff explained, "Ken Blanchard's book *One Minute Manager* talked about providing one-minute affirmations and critiques. First, we must recognize that a banquet or two a year, several thank-you notes or e-mails, public recognition from the pulpit, flowers, a gift, a personalized T-shirt or hat—these are all great ideas for making the most of small and large victories in the process of quality improvement. Nevertheless, as ministry team leaders learn the principle of celebration and critique, they will take time to meet after an event to team build and to affirm participants. When quality improvement becomes a part of our personal and church culture, we can expect such review. If we drop the ball, we can expect to get loving, direct and specific attention. Everything is placed in a context of How can we do better next time?"

Beth interjected, "Sounds like accountability."

"Yes," Jeff replied, "team members get frustrated if we do not hold people accountable. We need to ask questions such as: What happened last Sunday when we had all that dead time between the servicing of communion elements? Sometimes you may even need to talk to a person who may be a consistent problem. However, in most instances, you will work with the whole team on improving quality performance."

Gary nodded and noted, "The critique is not a scolding?"

"As long as motives and intent seem to be positive, no," responded Jeff. "If there is a motive to hurt or ruin a project, that person needs to be taken aside and lovingly questioned about his or her perceived motives. Remember, our goal is quality relationships, not just quality ministry and products."

"That can be a tough thing to remember when you're in the middle of a conflict or discrepancy," Beth added.

"Again, people skills are significant," said Jeff, "but the ability to work with each other becomes an opportunity to grow ourselves. We learn to love, accept and forgive those on our team who may not feel the way we feel about an idea. Just as grace must be balanced by justice, our celebrations of improvement must be balanced by the appropriate confrontation over discrepancies."

Jeff continued, "I'm not sure whether the lack of a quality improvement process means you won't have any quality outcomes. What I do know is, excellent or talented individuals can perform quality ministry, but they do it alone. That is not our goal. We want to develop a team. We don't need a church, or in my case a hotel staff, of prima donnas who use people and eat up others in the process."

"That goes back to the vine passage," Gary observed. "If we abide, we will bear fruit. If we don't abide, our fruit becomes few and false—like hanging plastic apples on an apple tree."

"Good illustration," Jeff remarked. "We want natural, organic quality that is lovingly nurtured with hard work. We may not be able to become a five-star church if we do these things. There are no guarantees. But I can tell you that we will not become a five-star church without this emphasis."

Well done is better than well said.

— BEN FRANKLIN

THE GIST OF IT...
WHY WE DO WHAT WE DO AND THE WAY WE DO IT

The goal of this chapter is to understand that the goal of quality concern is not so much a product as it is a process. In other words, the process is our primary goal.

The temptation of any task-oriented group is to focus on the task at hand and get it done as efficiently as possible. When effectiveness is a higher objective, however, quality concern must be part of the formula. A quality-improvement system is like the wiring or plumbing of a house. Installing it initially is a lot of effort, but once it is up and running, we can use it regularly without significant attention and enjoy the benefits.

Many times, we tend to assume that we are communicating more than we really are. The goal is proactive discussion versus reactive criticism. Waiting for someone to complain before taking action can cause you to lose people who do not want to say anything. This sometimes happens in a church because people do not want to be perceived as negative and may not feel the right to complain as compared to purchasing a tangible product.

Newcomers rarely volunteer information that is critical, but then they are also not apt to return if their needs are not met. The flip side is, regular church attendees complain more in a church than they would at a store or business because churches tend to be more like families. When they care more, they complain more.

We facilitate safe idea sharing by inviting comments from all the people in ministry and not just the directors and coordinators. Don't rely solely on the ministry leaders to ask their ministry members for constructive appraisal. The nature of politics and the potential for hurt feelings among ministry laypeople and the leadership inhibits honest and objective responses. The best method is to solicit feedback anonymously or by having a third party ask sensitive questions. Any other method presents the temptation to deny a problem.

Do we ask nursery parents how they liked the nursery staff and the facilities? Have we asked them how they liked the check-in and checkout policies, cleanliness, crafts, snacks and lesson time? How do we measure this sort of feedback? How often do we gather it? What do we do with the information after it is gathered? Who collects, keeps and analyzes it?

Giving people a reason to stay a few minutes for a stand-up meeting or gathering them within the week of a special event with the promise of food are ideas for developing feedback.

QUESTIONS AND ANSWERS

Q. Come on, you're talking about bogging down every meeting with laborious critiques.

Alan: The idea is not to strangle meetings. When quality becomes a high priority, it naturally pops up in our conversations and agendas. Just as most of us pray because we consider prayer a priority, so a simple focus on the quality issue is enough.

Quality will probably need to be an intentional agenda item until the process gets established. Then the emphasis will, by nature, include a concern for quality, and events or programs that do not reflect the quality of excellence will call attention to themselves.

Stan: I have found great success in church board meetings during the closing 15 minutes of the meeting. I always give my senior pastor/pastoral staff a report during that time, and during those moments I communicate quality concepts and, of course, excellence as a process. I have also tried to convey to every leader, Don't have a meeting unless you have a reason to meet.

Excellence is not a policy decision. It is a mind-set,
an attitude, a way of thinking and behaving.
We create a mind-set of excellence in our businesses,
our sports teams, our churches, and our homes
not merely by demanding excellence,
but by modeling excellence.

— A N O N Y M O U S

Q. As the senior pastor, I can determine this quality discussion in my ministry areas, but how do I make sure this quality talk takes place among other ministry directors or among my staff?

Stan: I use three basic steps to encourage the quality-driven church:

1. Prepare prayerfully.
2. Plan ahead.
3. Communicate positively.

KEYS TO EXCELLENCE AT TRINITY CHURCH

As a leader, I have attempted to communicate the following to the Trinity Church family:

- We must possess a passion for excellence.
- We are a learning organization.
- We must never settle for mediocrity.
- We must strive to glorify God.
- We must live out the Golden Rule.
- We will give people an opportunity to minister.
- We understand that humans will fail.
- We will strive to win our community to Christ.

Alan: The key is training and accountability. As a ministry leader, it is your responsibility to be sure quality is a matter of concern. Proper initial training, team discussion of benchmarks and measuring feedback from ministry users are ways of making sure quality gets more than just a token nod.

Gathering feedback surveys, interviews, and looking for growth data are like checking the dipstick of your car oil. How are we doing? If there have been some problems, or if you're making some quality changes, then check up more frequently than when things are going well. New people usually need more monitoring at the beginning to see how they are adding or deleting from the pursuit of excellence.

Q. How do I inspect without putting people on the defensive or making them think, *I'm a volunteer—why should I have to put up with these standards?*

Alan: Our job, initially, is to help people understand why we do what we do. Because more people than ever have a consumer-quality orientation, explaining this is easier now than ever. You can use examples of restaurants, grocery stores and retailers when it comes to people's desire for excellence.

Stan: For years, I have practiced MBO (Ministry by Objectives) through the use of the RIGs Program. RIGs stands for Responsibilities, Indicators, Goals. To achieve excellence in ministry, I have attempted to clearly inform leaders of their responsibilities as indicated in the following diagram and then challenge them to establish ministry goals that connect with our church's vision plan.

TRINITY CHURCH RIGs PROGRAMMER

Stewardship Team Leader   Date_____   Indicators_____

Duties	GOAL	May	June	July	Aug	Sept	Oct	Nov	Dec	Jan	Feb	Mar	Apr
Appoint Ministry Action Team (MAT)	N/A						✓	✓	✓	✓			
Select a Theme	N/A						✓						
Order Envelopes	250							✓					
Prepare Stewardship Leters	250							✓					
Commitment Cards	250							✓					
Partnership with God	250								✓				
Weekly Handouts	250								✓				
Stewardship Testimonies	4								✓	✓			
Family Giving Units	10									(11)VPTL			

Q. How far do I go in confronting discrepancies in ministry expectations? After all, we're doing our best and most of our people are volunteers. Won't I lose my workers if I start bringing up inadequacies in our ministries?

Stan: We must never forget that people will fail. They're human beings. I believe we must empower, release and call for accountability. When they fail, pray with them, assure them and encourage them. If things do not improve, then appoint someone else to lead their ministry area.

Alan: Knowing how far to go with confronting a discrepancy is always a subjective call. You have to ask questions: *Am I willing to lose this person if he or she gets upset? Do I have others who could replace him or her?* It means possessing competent people skills that allow you to discuss honest, but needed, changes of behavior and attitude.

A leader must also ask himself, *Is this a big deal?* If it is not, don't treat it like one, but make brief mention of it. Is it enough to remind the team of the ministry standards to avoid anyone feeling picked on, or is it better to pull a single team member aside for a dialogue?

Assume that you are part of the blame whenever quality does not take place. Perhaps it was poor communication or training. Never assume that the team member had the wrong motives. Every situation is different, but if you do nothing, quality will suffer and team members who are responding well can resent the lack of equity in keeping standards high.

THE DOERS SECTION

- How do we feel about the concept of the vine and fruitfulness?
- What can we do to model the environment for safe idea sharing in our staff and ministries meetings?
- How can we measure our progress?
- How do we discuss quality issues in our ministry?

- How will we gather dated feedback from ministry participants?
- What will we do with this information?
- How can we clarify our expectations for various ministry events?
- How will we measure our effectiveness after events or programs?
- What can we do to lovingly confront discrepancies in what we do and say?
- How can we celebrate quality ministry and improvements?

The quality of a person's life is in direct proportion to their commitment to excellence, regardless of their chosen field of endeavor.

—VINCE LOMBARDI
GREEN BAY PACKERS COACH

RATE YOUR CHURCH

Circle Your Response
1. Very Weak   2. Weak   3. Mediocre   4. Strong   5. Very Strong

A five-star church communicates well:

Our church has a written vision statement	1	2	3	4	5
Church members have a copy of our vision statement	1	2	3	4	5
Our vision statement is given to all new members	1	2	3	4	5
Our vision statement is reviewed at least annually	1	2	3	4	5
Our vision is clearly communicated to our membership	1	2	3	4	5

A five-star church is willing to make necessary changes:

Our church is open to change	1	2	3	4	5
Our church does not cling to ineffective ministries	1	2	3	4	5

Our church is not strapped by tradition   1 2 3 4 5
Our church organization is flexible   1 2 3 4 5
Our church looks more to the future than to the past   1 2 3 4 5

A five-star church develops exciting goals:

Our church has written goals   1 2 3 4 5
We review the progress on our goals at least annually   1 2 3 4 5
Our leadership understands the goals   1 2 3 4 5
Our goals are measurable   1 2 3 4 5
Our goals are realistic   1 2 3 4 5

A five-star church has a strategic action plan:

We have a strategy that is working for reaching people   1 2 3 4 5
We have a strategy for assimilating people into our church 1 2 3 4 5
We have a strategy for spiritual growth   1 2 3 4 5
We have a strategy for developing leaders   1 2 3 4 5
Our strategies match the resources of our church   1 2 3 4 5

A five-star church challenges every member to minister:

Members of our church understand and   1 2 3 4 5
use their spiritual gifts
Members see themselves as lay ministers   1 2 3 4 5
Our church effectively helps people find their   1 2 3 4 5
places in ministry
Laypersons are empowered and equipped to minister   1 2 3 4 5
The pastor and staff equip the laity for ministry   1 2 3 4 5

A five-star church effectively cares for the needs of people:

Laypersons are trained to do pastoral care   1 2 3 4 5
Laypersons are the primary caregivers   1 2 3 4 5
Members know where to turn in a time of need   1 2 3 4 5
Meaningful relationships are easily developed in our church 1 2 3 4 5
Most members are part of a small group   1 2 3 4 5

Developing Quality Teams

★ ★ ★ ★ ★

*Building an effective team depends on putting the
right people in the right place.*

— L A R R Y   G I L B E R T

Three weeks had passed since Beth, Gary and Jeff had met to discuss
their five-star church. Jeff had been out of town for a conference
and then vacation, so the trio had postponed a few of their training
sessions. Gary and Beth had worked hard to implement the ideas
Jeff had taught them. Progress was being made, but they were
beginning to experience some bumps in the road.

Inside the hotel lobby, Gary and Beth sat comfortably as Jeff
approached with a handshake and a grin.

Gary smiled. "Welcome back, Jeff. How did your conference go?"

"It was terrific," Jeff nodded as he sat down beside them. "We
really learned a lot about enhancing customer service."

"Were you there to learn or to present?" Beth asked.

"Both," Jeff responded. "One thing about quality improvement is
that you're always learning something. As soon as you think you've
got something mastered, the market changes, or the competition
tries harder. If you let your guard down, you are in danger of
becoming mediocre."

"I hope your vacation went well," Gary offered.

"It was terrific," said Jeff. "While you were back here slaving away, I was on the beach getting a suntan."

"Who took over when you were gone?" asked Gary. "This is a big operation for you to walk away from."

"It is, but we do most of our work in teams. The staff hardly notices when I'm away. Which leads me to the topic of the day: working in teams as opposed to having individual leaders. This is important because quality improvement will not happen unless you work in teams."

"Most churches function by committees," Gary noted. "What's the difference between a team and a committee?"

Jeff was emphatic. "Night and day! Let's start with motivation. There is a much broader and deeper sense of ownership when people develop a team approach. This approach contrasts sharply against the conventional committee where the chairperson is the main planner."

"In other words," Beth added, "two heads are better than one."

"And three or more heads are better than two," said Jeff, following up her point. "Research shows very clearly that the more people are involved in a process, the higher the caliber of ideas that get generated. By bringing up an idea in a group, you have the opportunity to polish it. How many great ideas have failed miserably because some corporate president had a brainstorm but was out of touch with the trenches—the people doing and using the product or service?"

"Sounds like a typical church," Gary commented.

"Churches are," Jeff explained, "in many ways, like any other organization in how they are structured and deal with people. We have to get away from the idea that only a few trained professionals, or even a small group of volunteers and paid leaders, can generate the number and quality of ideas necessary to constantly improve ministry."

"Jeff," Beth asked, "why have so many organizations moved toward teams? Is it just a temporary fad?"

"It's not a fad, Beth. One reason is that now, more than any time in the past, people are better educated. Education tends to make people want to participate in the process instead of being told what to do by some factory foreman."

Jeff motioned with his hands and continued, "Another reason is competition. In the past, if you had a good product or service, you could often corner the market. But now, with more rapid change and fast competition, we need people who'll help in the process because more heads are better than one."

"Makes sense," Gary replied.

Jeff nodded. "Yes, and another reason I think we're seeing teams replacing committees is that the boomers and gen-Xers are more experiential: They want to participate, make a difference, and see their ideas acted upon. These main reasons have created a social movement away from traditional committees toward teams."

"Jeff, help me understand the difference between teams and committees again," said Beth. "I suppose you could call a committee a team and still have it function like a committee."

Jeff laughed. "Organizational fads have a way of changing our language without changing our behavior. Here's a quick overview. I think I have a chart here that lists some of the basic differences between committees and teams."

Jeff pushed a button on the computer, and a chart appeared on the wall. "Committees tend to be more passive; teams are more active. Committee members tend to be selected by others via election or selection. Team members are selected for their involvement. Committees meet periodically, with or without new information. Teams meet as needed and only exist so long as there is a task to perform. Committees tend to defer action to others. Teams tend to deploy the actions they develop. Committees tend to be managerial in nature and tend toward maintaining and making incremental changes. Teams tend to be leadership oriented and can perform significant changes if needed."

"Yes," Gary interjected, "but how do we get away from the committee mentality? For a long time it has been part of our history."

"You can talk about the benefits of teams," Jeff responded, "and work with your committee heads regarding training. However, I think the easiest way is to start with new teams. I'd use this new emphasis on quality improvement to also introduce the concept of teamwork at Family Church. Bundle it together."

"I'm getting a feel for the differences," Gary nodded, "but tell me more about why teams are more effective. What do teams have to do with the quality-improvement process?"

"You're asking the right questions," Jeff pointed out. "Quality improvement is based on the idea that everyone has an opinion and a good idea on how things can run. Your people who actually do the ministry hear the requests from the ministry users, and they also know if things are working as they should. Some of them may be part of the problem, but they are also part of the solution."

Beth chipped in, "Another benefit of teams is that when everyone participates, you are more likely to see the ideas implemented. Everyone knows the frustration of not seeing the improvement ideas fleshed out after they're generated."

"The word we're looking for is 'ownership,'" said Jeff. "True ownership comes when the team generates the ideas and seeks to implement them, not when a couple of people generate the ideas and suggest that the team members carry them out, with or without discussion."

The pastor smiled. "It's kind of like the difference between the hireling and the sheep owners in the biblical illustration. The hirelings tend to run at the first sign of danger."

"Nice connection, Gary," said Jeff. "We want the team members to own the ministry and the ideas they generate. If they do not have ownership, there will always be a significant lapse between what should be and what is—especially in a nonprofit organization."

Beth asked, "What's nonprofit got to do with it?"

"Let me explain," said Jeff. "At Majesty Suites, we have the leverage of employment, salary and benefits. In volunteer organizations, people tend to be motivated by issues other than money. They are looking for fulfillment and personal satisfaction. We motivate people differently in the Church than we do in the typical corporation because we cannot assume behavior will change for fear of being fired or demoted."

Gary folded his hands together and nodded in agreement. "The motivation factor is one issue we're struggling with now at Family Church. I don't want to sound like I'm complaining—we have wonderful people there. Yet it seems we often lack the motivation to implement these principles."

"That's where vision and teaching come into play," Jeff replied. "One benefit a faith community has over a corporation is that loyalty runs deeper. What we do becomes a matter of the soul. It is not just a career or checking account. If we can get our ministry directors to cast the vision for their individual ministries, we will have motivated people."

Gary sat back, folded his arms and sighed, "I've been trying to do too much of the ministry on my own and too much via committees."

"Committees are not bad," Jeff commented, "but they are not designed to create the sort of fruitfulness that a team can. Just as an apple tree cannot produce pears, so committees cannot create the same sort of excitement a well-run team can."

Gary questioned, "Still, don't we need some committees to take care of our church governmental structures?"

"Sometimes you need them for fiduciary responsibilities," said Jeff, "but teams can serve the same functions and better. You just don't meet to be meeting. If you have to gather regularly to record minutes, have a five-minute stand-up meeting. Keep it short and adjourn quickly. You don't need to soak up another night away from the family."

Inflexibility is one of the worst human failings. You can learn to check impetuosity, overcome fear with

confidence and laziness with discipline. But for
rigidity of mind there is no antidote. It carries the
seeds of its own destruction.

— A N O N Y M O U S

THE GIST OF IT...
WHY WE DO WHAT WE DO AND THE WAY WE DO IT

Times have changed. What turned the cranks of organizations at the turn of the twentieth century does not do so today. The concept of committee leadership is a product of slower-paced managerial organizations. As people and times change, so do the organizations that naturally reflect them.

Unfortunately, most churches are mired in a 1950s organizational structure and are quickly losing touch with the cultures in which they minister. Antiquated methods cannot keep pace with such drastic social changes. Our goal is not to conform to the world, but rather to do what is necessary to win a few, as Paul suggested.

Teams make quicker decisions and involve more members—creating efficient implementation. They tend to be less bureaucratic or managerial in nature. Teams thrive on tasks, not meetings. Because they are more task oriented than committees, they often meet less and usually for shorter periods, focusing more on participatory problem solving.

Ecclesiastes 4:9,10 says, "Two are better than one, because they have a good return for their work: If one falls down, his friend can help him up. But pity the man who falls and has no one to help him up!" The goal is to get the people involved in the ministry together to problem solve. This is a better system than to use those who may be elected to oversee an area but who are not actually involved in the area of ministry. In quality improvement, the goal is to gather input from a group of participants, not just overseers. Ideas generated from the inside are more likely to be practical and implement-ed than those created from the outside.

Another difference in using teams is that they invest a signifi-cant amount of time in building relationships. Getting to know people, sharing stories, discussing burdens and joys, praying together and just spending time together are key components in team building. Committees tend to stick to the business at hand, which usually does not include team-building exercises.

Team building has a lot to do with community building, which is a high priority in Christianity. How unfortunate that so many committee meetings result merely in getting through the agenda. Members come and go without anyone taking time to ask how they are doing, to see if they need personal prayer and to share their lives with each other.

Naturally, you cannot invest all meetings in team-building activities, or you won't get anything done. However, an annual retreat, a 15-minute huddle time with prayer and sharing and a 15-minute leader lesson or teamwork game goes a long way in long-term productivity. When relationships are strong, the team is willing to work through critical issues involving change. When people enjoy working together, they can overlook the periodic pain that results in constructive criticism, which is essential to the improvement process.

In other words, by enhancing team community, we increase the social and emotional rewards for participating. This is a vital ele-ment in volunteer organizations in which monetary pay is low or nonexistent. People are willing to donate their time and talent, but they want it to be enjoyable and fulfilling in the process. They want more than just a job; they want a community.

Good team leaders seek to understand what
motivates team members.

— S T A N   T O L E R

QUESTIONS AND ANSWERS

Q. Okay, I'm in a very seasoned, traditional church. What can I do to begin to introduce the team concept into my committee-laden congregation?

Stan: Because I am serving a church that has a long, successful history, I have taken baby steps to overcome any traditions that might hinder the future growth of the congregation.

During my first year as pastor, I began to talk about forming a ministry partnership. At each church board meeting, I shared my vision for the team-ministry concept. I also discussed spiritual gifts as the spiritual foundation for team building. Fortunately, the board was ready to make the changes quickly.

Some of the topics I covered with the church board were as follows:

1. Effective ministry teams are biblically based.
2. Effective ministry teams perform in the power of the Holy Spirit.
3. Effective ministry teams plan according to God's will.
4. Effective ministry teams pray together.
5. Effective ministry teams agree to move forward through consensus.

Modeling
is leadership validating itself.
Multiplying
is leadership fashioning its future.
Managing
is leadership conserving its strength.
Ministry
is leadership passing on its life.

—Harold L. Longenecker

Alan: I pastor a new, team-oriented congregation. But I have been on staff at a large church, laden with tradition and a managerial, committee process. The first thing I did was to include team-building activities in the committee meetings. I broke down some of the stiff, businesslike feel that committees often favor, and I began strengthening relationships.

If you attempt this same approach, you may need to explain the importance of this because some members may think you're just wasting their time with chitchat and touchy-feely stuff. Make sure you're focused, but start appropriately and increase the team-building activities as you go. Many businesspeople on your committees will be familiar with team-building processes.

Q. When they do, where do you think teams fail?

Alan: The number-one area of failure is in leadership development (discussed in the next chapter). Perhaps the next most overlooked area is in developing team spirit—*esprit de corps.*

Team leaders facilitate good communication by
responding to the information needs of the
organization.

— ALAN NELSON

Q. What is the best way to begin implementing teams in our church if we have not done it much in the past?

Stan: The pastoral leadership team should begin by teaching qualities that exemplify team excellence. Words such as "discipline," "courage," "perseverance," "vision" and "faith" should be used frequently in team meetings.

My pattern has been to seek the "blessing" of the existing church board to study the team-ministry concept. I have found churches very responsive to that approach. Next, I take a listening posture with all team leaders. I meet with them individually and then with their ministry action teams. I usually ask a staff member to be present to record notes from each meeting. Once I have received feedback, the journey to implementation begins.

Alan: There isn't a one-size-fits-all solution. Every church is different. You have to ask: How tradition bound is this congregation? Is the pastor a strong enough leader to cast the vision for the format change? Are there leaders available who can influence changes in style?

Almost regardless of the situation, the best single way to implement a team philosophy is through new groups. By building new wineskins, you need not change the old wineskins. You'll probably have to lay down some new ground rules in how these teams will run, especially if you're steeped in traditional committee structure. You'll need to make sure there are elements of team building, task assignments and accountability, and avoid managerial practices that are often a waste of time.

Starting a team approach with new groups allows you to nurture the team concept without trying to change existing committee routines. Once the team approach is cultivated, most people will prefer it.

Q. Again, what do teams have to do with quality improvement?

Alan: Working in teams is crucial to quality improvement because:

1. It enhances communication effectiveness, which is necessary to share and hone ideas.
2. It creates broader ownership among those who are participating and implementing.
3. It tends to enhance meeting effectiveness and efficiency in a situation when wasting time through meetings is discouraging.
4. It is more rewarding for generations where education and experience make participation a priority.
5. It better models Christian community in our task meetings.

6. It develops people as they participate, leaving them more valuable and experienced at the end of their group experience.

THE DOERS SECTION

- How is our church structured?
- Do we function as committees or ministry action teams?
- If we could restructure the entire church, what would it look like?
- Are any ministries or groups currently functioning as teams rather than committees?
- How can we change the way our ministries operate without a complete renovation?
- How could we transform our existing committees so they function more like teams?
- How would this new transformation affect our current organizational flowchart?
- What are the challenges of turning committees into ministry action teams?
- What are the potential benefits if our committees function like teams?
- What does quality improvement have to do with team building?
- Can you think of any examples where ideas generated by teams or groups created very positive results?

Creativity is finding new things...or expressing old truths in new ways.

—ROGER VAN GOECHE

Chapter
6

Developing Team Members
and Leaders

★ ★ ★ ★ ★

Leadership is the ability to organize the
spiritual gifts and limitations of others.

—J. OSWALD SANDERS

Beth and Gary were bursting with smiles and conversation as they waited in Jeff's hotel office. As the general manager of the Majesty Suites Hotel walked in and sat across from his friends, Jeff wasted no time in his greeting. "I know why you're excited. Today we're going to explore the critical role of team leaders."

Beth folded her hands and half smiled. "Well Jeff, you've been telling us for several weeks that this is a crucial part in building a five-star church. We're all ears."

The manager nodded. "I think that the nonprofit organization is the most leadership-intensive organization of all because of the unique work and motivation dynamics. But developing quality teams has a lot to do with who is on the team to begin with and, most importantly, who is the team leader."

Gary sat back in his chair and pulled out his pen and pad. "Please Jeff, let's talk about that."

"At Family Church," Jeff began, "I know that we emphasize the importance of people getting involved in a ministry. We do a good job finding a place for each person. We do basically the same thing at Majesty Suites. We don't put a restaurant manager in charge of changing the beds, and we don't hire someone interested in security as a front-desk person. We all have distinct roles. At Majesty Suites, there's no such thing as a wrong person, only a wrong job. As for churches, it's the leader's job to match a ministry to the person, not the other way around. Quality suffers when you have the right people in the wrong positions."

"Motivation suffers, too," Gary commented.

"Right," Jeff agreed. "Another thing that I have found helpful is measuring quotients. Research has shown that people have multiple areas of potential. Unfortunately, standard IQ tests only measure a couple of areas. Understanding quotients helps you paint a better portrait of your team members."

Gary asked, "Are you saying that we need to start giving IQ tests prior to ministry assignment?"

"I don't think that would go over well," Jeff laughed. "But acknowledging the fact that intellectual capacity is a factor in team roles will help us create more effective teams. For example, a high IQ person is apt to be bored quickly if he is not challenged to think. A higher IQ person may be looking for a break from a stressful job through a simple ministry role, but you'll be leaving a lot of potential on the table if you never tap that intellect. At the same time, a person with a lower IQ might feel overwhelmed if asked to perform a ministry that involves more complexity."

"Good, that makes sense," said Gary, relieved.

"Briefly, here are the others," said Jeff. "AQ stands for attitude quotient. A person with a high AQ is very positive. This person is a joy to have around. This person is not intimidated by circumstances or negative people, and tends to be pretty resilient to stress. Low AQ people are easily intimidated by situations and tend to complain easily. Never ask a low AQ to serve in a role of influence. It will sour the team."

"Bingo," said Beth. "The last thing we need is more sour people representing God."

Jeff moved on. "RQ represents resource quotient. In a church context, resources can include time, talent or treasure. People with a high-time resource can give a lot to ministry, so long as they're motivated and matched well. Talent has to do with a person's gifts. Treasure resources have to do with a person's ability to provide money or helpful networks of contacts. Kind of like Radar O'Reilly on the TV series "MASH," this person can always come up with the right thing at the right time."

Gary was surprised. "You mean that different people have different resource quotients and we should put them on teams appropriately?"

"Exactly," Jeff said. "You don't put your shortest guy at center on a basketball team. The best teams use people according to their strengths, not their weaknesses."

"Okay," Gary agreed, "what's the next quotient, Jeff?"

"It's EQ, which stands for energy quotient. Some people are high-capacity people in how they are wired. High-capacity people can fulfill multiple roles inside and outside the church. If you ask a low-capacity person to do more than a single ministry role, you'll overwhelm him, and quality and motivation will plummet. If you underutilize a high-capacity person, he'll get bored or feel he really is not needed."

"It seems that some of these work together," Beth opined. "For example, if you have a high-capacity person with limited time resources, you can overburden her with church work."

"Good point, Beth," said Jeff. "They do work together. The goal is to help your ministry leaders understand this when putting together a ministry team. One more thing they need to know about is the last quotient, which is MQ, or motivation quotient. This may be the most important quotient because it engages or disengages all the others. A person who is highly motivated will tend to get involved with his other talents, resources and abilities. When you think of it, Jesus put a lot of stock in high MQ people. He wanted to know whether they were willing to pay the price required to follow Him."

"That's true," said Gary. "I can think of the person in the Bible who would not give his wealth to the poor."

"The Bible is full of stories based on motivation," Jeff replied. "The greatest frustration has to be in seeing such great potential just sit week after week, inactive, unmotivated."

"So how do we motivate?" Gary asked.

"Ultimately, you can't," said Jeff, shaking his head. "All you can do is strive to provide an environment in which people can be self-motivated. You can cast the vision, give pep talks, teach and train, and place people in the right ministry, but the bottom line is their free will. You can't *make* people get involved."

"You know," Gary raised a finger, "I'd include one more quotient for ministry teams. That would be SQ for spirituality quotient."

Beth asked, "Why that?"

"Well," Gary explained, "there are numerous roles where you have to consider a person's maturity in the faith. For example, leaders need to be spiritually mature because of their roles as models and decision makers. Although some roles do not *require* spiritual maturity, it seems that we need to consider people's SQ before inviting them to ministry roles that may overwhelm them."

"Great point," said Jeff. "You could come up with other quotients pertinent to your specific teams, but these are some of the basics."

Beth glanced at her notes quietly. Her expression was pensive. Jeff paused and inquired gently, "Beth, are you okay?"

"Yes, I'm fine," she said.

Jeff added, "Generally, you've been pretty quiet today."

"I'm sorry," she replied, "I've been thinking about why we aren't seeing more of our teams take off with these principles. When we've talked about them in groups, people seem to catch the concepts and nod their heads affirmingly. They are all well-intentioned people, but many of the ministry groups don't seem to be running with our training at this point. It's as if we're missing a key to the ignition."

"Let me tell you what I believe is the key to developing effective quality teams," said Jeff. "Teams are catalyzed by team leaders. If you're having a team motivation problem, 9 times out of 10 it's really just a leadership problem. No position is more crucial than the team leader."

"If so, Jeff, where have we gone wrong?"

"Beth, I'm not sure if we've gone wrong. Remember, the goal of quality improvement is to be focused on what you can do better next time. I think there are some areas where teams can go wrong in leadership selection because committees tend to naturally select managers. People who are managers tend not to feel comfortable with leadership issues that include team building."

Beth asked, "So where do you find team-building leaders, Jeff?"

The manager smiled. "In most leadership roles today you need people who are evenly weighted between getting things done and building relationships. Old-style leading used to be task oriented, but not necessarily user friendly to team members. If you get someone that's too task oriented, he may accomplish the job, but no one will enjoy the process. Turnover will be high. That doesn't work well, especially in a faith community. Conversely, if you get a superb people-person who is not task oriented, your team will have a wonderful time, but they won't accomplish much."

"That makes sense," Beth said. "As you explain that, people quickly come to mind who are too task oriented or too people oriented. Are the types of leaders we are looking for born or made?"

"Laboratory experiments being the exception, these types of leaders are born," Jeff said.

The trio laughed.

"Seriously," Jeff continued, "we need to look for people who have spiritual maturity because we're a faith community. We also need to look for people who have had past leadership roles in school, work and the community."

"How do we create a larger pool from which to draw?" Gary asked.

"I think that one of the best ways is to have coleaders in every ministry area," Jeff responded. "Not only does this relieve the potential stress of a single person doing the job, but it also makes sure the bases are covered if the person is gone or leaves for whatever reason. All the while you're developing twice as many potential leaders compared with only having one leader in every ministry."

Beth interjected, "So how do you get rid of current ministry leaders who really are not leaders?"

"You fire them," Jeff deadpanned.

The three friends laughed again.

As the laughter subsided, Jeff explained, "I'm kidding to a point, but this is a challenge. It's tough to fire a volunteer. However, if we are to take a quality-improvement mind-set, we have to elevate the good of the church body over simple acceptance of poor leadership. As we incorporate a quality-improvement culture at Family Church, it will be easier to change staff because we'll be used to changing other things too. Moreover, we should incorporate written job descriptions of the ministry which have a specific time commitment included. When the time commitment is completed, it offers the church a natural transition to employ any stronger team leader who has emerged."

"That's a great idea," said Beth. "People might also be more inclined to stick with a ministry for a given period of time if they know there is a natural ending date."

Gary added, "They might also be more inclined to sign up for a ministry team as well! Churches are notorious for having open-ended, till-we-rapture-in-the-sky ministry mind-set."

"Think about this biblical example," Jeff said. "Jethro advised his son-in-law, Moses, to quit trying to do all the ministry himself and to develop people who could oversee groups of 10, 50, 100 and 1,000. Different leaders have different levels of ability and influence. Just because a person is good at one level does not mean he or she will be as good at a higher level of influence. Sometimes you can only learn this by trial. Give people a chance. The leader's job is to develop other leaders and to empower and unleash them."

Only those who dare to fail greatly
can ever achieve greatly.

—ROBERT KENNEDY

THE GIST OF IT...
WHY WE DO WHAT WE DO AND THE WAY WE DO IT

Quality improvement in ministry demands the functioning of healthy teams. Healthy teams require that members and leaders be in the right roles and proportions.

When a group lacks quality leadership, it will tend to languish. Leadership is a social construct. No one leads by himself. In recent years, the popularity in the concept of leadership has sparked numerous articles and book titles. Many of these publications imply that everyone can be a leader and that a person even can lead without followers.

Leading yourself is little more than self-discipline, hardly the same as social leading. If everyone were a leader, then life would be even more chaotic. No, God gives His Body the right parts; some are teachers, some counselors, some evangelists and a few leaders.

Leadership is one part of a category we might call supervision. A supervisor refers to a person who is most responsible for a group. A person who is a supervisor may not be a leader. He may be a manager or administrator. We commonly misperceive that because a person is assigned the head of the table in a committee meeting, or is elected as a committee chair, or is the pastor of the church, then that person is the leader. In the common sense of the term, he is. In the specific sense, he may not be. Position does not make a person a leader—leadership does.

In a similar sense, everything a leader does is not leading. Sometimes, leaders are actually managers, parents, servants, teachers and followers, depending on their behavior at the moment. We assume that leaders are people who lead at the appropriate time, when leading is needed.

Involving people in the right roles is one of the first objectives of any team. You cannot overlook the importance of investigating what it takes to accomplish a certain ministry effectively and then finding individuals who have those resources. For example, what do you need to make people feel at home in God's house, which is the ministry of hospitality? You will probably want an outgoing, people-oriented person rather than an introverted, task-oriented individual. What does it take to effectively teach a class of third graders? What gifts and skills are needed to serve on a church board?

Sometimes this process happens through the Holy Spirit in spite of our lack of procedures and, occasionally, it occurs intuitively. If we could hone our techniques to use the Spirit, intuition and a methodical aptitude-discovery process, we could raise our average. Think about it: The difference between a gold medal and a bronze medal in the Olympic Games is often several hundredths of a second. The difference between a mediocre ministry and one that excels is often just a little system improvement.

We owe it to people to help them find what they are good at doing. The shotgun approach to ministry-team selection must become a rifle method. This will not guarantee success, but it will significantly increase your chances and decrease your failure rate.

People want to be used by God. They want to find a place of significance in the world. The job of the congregational staff is to help them find this niche. The role of ministry involvement is on the rise as the lay ministry movement emerges into the twenty-first century.

How do you select people to serve on your teams? Do you recruit or do you invite people? True team participation ought to be perceived as an honor rather than an obligation. All this is to say that putting the right people on the right ministry team is essential for quality ministry improvement.

The most important part of quality ministry is getting the right leaders in the right places. Teams work best with vision, interaction and team building. Leaders are about change. Because quality improvement involves change, a person having some level of gifted leadership is necessary.

Leaders are catalysts. They perceive people quotients and build team spirit. They cast the vision to see the big picture in ministry improvement. They are willing to confront people and situations that block the benefit of the whole team and the pursuit of ministry improvement. Status quo is not a peaceful place for a true leader. Complacency in ministry contradicts a leader's spirit and a ministry-improvement philosophy, which is why leaders and quality improvement go hand in hand.

The style of leadership necessary to bring about effective team building is twenty-first century in nature, meaning that leading styles vary from leader to leader. The twentieth-century style—top down, autocratic, which has been commonly perceived as strong leadership—is detrimental to team building. This style creates an overdependency on the leader and suppresses idea sharing and teamwork that is necessary in quality-improvement teams.

At various times, a team will have different needs in leadership. A novice team will often require a hands-on approach. This contrasts with the needs of an experienced team focused on quality improvement. This mature team demands more freedom in projects because members feel capable and knowledgeable in carrying out their duties. In the latter case, a leader must let loose and become more laid back with the members.

Those leaders who cannot appropriately alter their leadership methods to match the needs of the team will become ineffective. As the group changes, the leader must either adapt to that change or seek out a new team. If the leader refuses to change their style of leadership or to seek out a group that needs their particular brand of leadership the team will become dysfunctional and its potential will not be reached.

Strong team members desire stronger leaders, but the strength is more a matter of confidence and competence than control and dominance. Generally, more educated and professional team members prefer a leadership style that is less dominant because they want more of a participatory role. A competent leader will sense that desire and adjust appropriately to the need.

The bottom line is that savvy team leaders will intuitively and consciously know the level and style of leading that a team needs to do its job. Teams that do not "get off the dime" tend to be ones in which those in charge are either not really leaders or have not caught the vision of what needs to happen on the team. Leader selection and development are primary steps in establishing quality-improvement ministry teams.

When you're through changing, you're through!

—BRUCE BARTON

QUESTIONS AND ANSWERS

Q. Placing people in the right place is one thing, but how do we get more people involved in ministry, period?

Alan: I would begin by sharing three basic ideas:

1. *There is no such thing as unmotivated people.*
   The same employee who grunts at work also dashes to his car after work to play on the softball team. One of the best ways to help people find motivation for ministry is to develop processes for discovering their interests and passions. If you can make a ministry tap into this passion, you're home free.

2. *It all comes down to vision casting.*

   When a ministry director comes to me and says she can't find people who want to get involved in her ministry, I lovingly suggest she hasn't shared the vision effectively or to the right people. When people see the eternal benefit of changing diapers, setting up chairs, or feeding the homeless—they'll want to get involved. Passion is contagious!

3. *Ask people to commit.*

   Surveys show that 80 percent of people, if asked, would get involved in ministry and service. The "task of ask" is an important aspect of leading. Leaders are sellers. Ministry fairs, worship folders and newsletter announcements are great, but *nothing* beats a personal invitation to consider a ministry opportunity.

Stan: One of the first steps for me at Trinity was to bring the leadership team together and discuss our vision plan. We agreed that Trinity had been built on relationships, so we created a vision acronym:

F Focus on relationships
R Renew our commitment
I Invite to participate
E Equip to minister
N Network the Body
D Demonstrate God's love
S Serve with gladness

Our next step was to invite our friends to be partners with us in ministry. Their involvement has ultimately resulted in reaching out to their friends and families.

Q. Everyone's talking about leadership these days. How are you using the term and how is this different from so many others who talk about it?

Stan: In my book *The People Principle: Transforming Laypersons into Leaders* (Kansas City, Missouri: Beacon Hill Press, 1997), I discuss three types of leaders:

1. The shepherd leader
2. The servant leader
3. The steward leader

I have chosen to focus on the steward leader approach because I think it combines the best qualities of the first two leadership styles. The steward leader is like a spiritual coach.

I teach the steward leaders in my church two critical areas of responsibility:

1. The stewardship of the mission and vision
2. The stewardship of the gifts of God's people

Peter Block's book *Stewardship* has captured the imagination of many marketplace leaders, but he used a biblical concept and transferred it to corporate America. To me, it was a no-brainer. This word, "stewardship," belongs to the Church. Let's reclaim it and utilize it in a scriptural manner with our leaders.

Alan: I'm pretty much a nut when it comes to defining the term, but my definition of leadership is "a process whereby people work together to bring about intended change by providing influence resources to individuals who serve as leaders." This fast overview helps you see that leadership is a social process, not just what leaders do.

The real power of leadership is in the group members. You can't lead someone who doesn't want to be led. That's called coercion. When a leader recognizes that his or her influence is regularly fluctuating in terms of group member motivation, confidence and personal objectives, the leader will better understand how some things do and do not get changed. The word "change" separates leading from managing. If we can make leading a smaller process and focus more on its unique qualities, we stand a better chance in understanding and improving it.

Q. Why is leadership so important to a team and to quality improvement? Why can't we do the same with committees and managers?

Alan: Leadership is vital to any organization that needs to undergo change. Quality Improvement is about constant change to improve service and product. Once the process is up and running smoothly, a managerial person can bring about incremental changes toward excellence. But for most of us in the church, we will need to make significant changes toward teamwork versus committees, and from business as usual to a cutting-edge, people-oriented ministry.

The whole concept of teams necessitates people who are adept at people skills and who can build ministry teams. The best way to develop and train other leaders is to find a few leaders and then have each of them mentor an associate. The associate then stands a better chance of succeeding. We rarely have any ministries in which only one person is the director. By using codirectors, you help people share the workload, and you're always developing new leaders for potential ministry positions. The team process itself is a good way to broaden and deepen the leadership ability in your congregation.

Stan: I often say to pastors, "Never go to the hospital alone." My reason is that pastors often have the "do it alone" mentality. If you involve people in ministry and take them along, you expand the caring base of your church greatly!

Q. What if I don't have enough leaders right now for every ministry team? Do I give up on the quality-improvement idea?

Stan: Thanks for asking that question. When I was planting a church in Tampa, Florida, I couldn't seem to attract adults in the early days of my ministry. Once, I decided to present a concert and invited a musical team to perform. As the event grew nearer, I realized I didn't have any ushers. I looked around for a friendly face, and the only one I could find was nine-year-old Walter Rutherford. He was a lover of people and hugged everyone!

On the day of the event, I placed Walter at the door, instructed him to shake hands with everyone and to introduce any new guests to me. I'll never forget what happened next. In a matter of moments I heard Walter yell out, "Preacher, preacher, preacher! We've got some new customers here today!" Startled, I looked around and sure enough, six brand-new adults came.

Often, small-church pastors tell me they don't have enough people to help, so I tell them to find the "Walters" in their congregation. Children can become excellent greeters.

Alan: Jesus emphasized the importance of availability. You may have several who like the idea, but for various reasons, aren't available to be involved. Let go of the disappointment! Get the ball rolling! You can help new people find their roles as team leaders. The leader's goal is to help create an atmosphere in which excellence is valued. The process will be long, but it will result in very tangible results that everyone will applaud.

Great ministry teams solve problems together.
— STAN TOLER

THE DOERS SECTION

- What groups, teams or ministries are currently functioning in our church?
- Do we have a written ministry inventory, including names of leaders and active participants?

- Rate each ministry on a scale of one to five: (1) needs a complete overhaul, (2) needs significant work, (3) needs a tune-up, (4) running well, and (5) zooming.
- What do we know about the leaders of the ministries that are languishing?
- What are we doing now to help church members find places of ministry in which their gifts are best utilized?
- What are other helpful leadership characteristics for team member placement?
- Who are potential team leaders who are either misplaced or not being used?
- What did we learn in this chapter about why leadership is so crucial to church-team development?
- How could we develop better leaders in our congregation?
- Discuss ways to position key influencers in ministry leadership roles.

Share ministry team success with celebrations.

—ALAN NELSON

Chapter
7

The Secret Church Shopper

✸ ✸ ✸ ✸ ✸

People don't care how much you know until
they know how much you care.

— HOWARD HENDRICKS

Jeff walked down the hall and into the attractive boardroom of the Majesty Suites Hotel, where notepads and ice water were set on a table. Beth and Gary were already seated, discussing how quality at Family Church was improving.

"Good morning," said Jeff with a chirp to his voice. "How are my partners doing?"

"We're just fine, Jeff," said Gary. "We can't wait to see what you have up your sleeve this week."

"Today, I have my arm up my sleeve," said Jeff, touching the left arm of his business suit. "No tricks, as you can see."

"I think we're seeing some significant improvements at Family Church in recent weeks," Beth began, "especially in the quality-improvement process. Our small groups are talking about how they can do things better, and we're beginning to see some tangible results."

"That's great news, Beth," said Jeff. "I'm so proud of the way you've cast the vision and how you're striving to raise the bar on quality. I've heard good reports in some of the ministry meetings I've been a part of."

"You've been so helpful, Jeff," Gary jumped in. "I can see us becoming a five-star church."

"Well, if you're serious about this ministry excellence thing, then I have an idea for you today," Jeff replied. "But I've got to warn you, it's not for the faint of heart."

"We're game," said Beth eagerly. "Fire away!"

"The idea is a secret church shopper."

"What's a secret church shopper?" asked Gary. "Besides, what's secret about church shopping? Seems like it's some people's favorite pastime these days."

"Every month, we have at least one secret hotel guest who pretends to be a customer and then rates us on the level of service, responsiveness and first impressions at Majesty Suites," said Jeff.

"I assume you do pretty well," Gary stated. "Everything seems to be perfect."

"Trust me; it's not," Jeff replied. "Hiring secret shoppers to come in and critique us can be a frustrating practice, but the small and big ideas they have generated have helped us create the quality service and atmosphere you mentioned."

Beth was curious. "Why would a church need this? Can't we generate enough ideas from our own people?"

"Human nature is funny, isn't it?" Jeff smiled. "Things that bother us at first become old hat and no big deal after a while. For example, your bathroom mirror cracks. The first week, it bugs you to death. Every day you think, *I've got to get that fixed.* The second week, you notice it, but you get busy with other things. By week three, you hardly notice the crack, and after a month or two, someone comes to your house and says, 'Did you know that your mirror is cracked?' You had forgotten. Obviously, that's a bit of an exaggeration, but you get the point. Our minds often overlook information that is familiar."

"Now we're back to the first impressions principle," Beth noted.

"That's true," said Jeff. "First impressions are huge for people stepping into a church for the first time. If they don't come back, they will rarely tell you why. If a family does return a few times, they will often forget the things that bugged them at first."

Beth asked, "Does this mean we should hire someone to come to Family Church and give us feedback on their first impressions?"

"That's pretty much it," said Jeff. "I've been trying to think of how we can translate what we do at Majesty Suites to church life, and it's not a big difference."

"Okay," Gary brightened, "how would we do it? I've never heard of a church intentionally implementing secret shoppers, but it sounds helpful. People shop all the time. We should be aware of what newcomers are seeing and feeling."

"Exactly," said Jeff. "We'll need to initially answer three questions—who, what and how. The *who* means finding a shopper who fits the profile of the type of person we're trying to attract. Since our goal is to attract the unchurched to Family Church, we will want to find someone outside of our church but who reflects the spiritual and social demographics of our target market."

"So if you're a younger church," Beth added, "you find a young adult. If you're a Hispanic congregation, get a Hispanic shopper."

"Right," said Jeff. "For some churches, this will really stretch them because they will discover they are not set up to attract people they say they are trying to reach. I don't think that will be a big deal at our church since we're pretty clear on who we are trying to reach."

Gary blinked. "Where do we find these shoppers?"

"Believe it or not, there are agencies that provide secret shoppers. Most are students, homemakers or retired people who can take the time to check out a bank or business. I don't think we need to spend the extra money to go that route, although it may be a good idea."

"I think we could easily find someone from the community or even a friend of someone from a neighboring church," said Gary.

"Again," Jeff nodded, "we need to make sure we get a person or family who truly represents the type of person we are striving to attract. Old-time churchgoers will look at our congregation in a significantly different fashion from a seeking person. I think we need to contact a person with perspective, but who is not overly critical or negative. The goal is first impressions and quality observation, not just picky criticism."

Beth asked, "Jeff, do we pay them?"

"Yes, we do. If you want this to be a professional experience and for people to say yes, you have to pay them. I think $25 to $75 would be a typical pay range, depending on how much feedback you desire from them."

"Paying people to come to church," grinned Gary. "Wait till that word gets out."

"Wait a minute, pastor," said Beth. "They pay *you* to come to church."

"Okay, that's enough," Gary replied.

Jeff offered, "I could probably find plenty of shoppers through my network here and in the community. I'll be glad to train those people, too. The next issue is deciding what we'll want feedback on."

Gary asked, "So we're not just interested in generic first impressions?"

"Yes," Jeff explained, "but we'll also want to target a few ministry areas for feedback purposes. For example, if you want to know how we're doing in our nursery, we need to find a shopper who has an infant or toddler and have that mother actually use the nursery. We want feedback on the nursery staff, cleanliness, security system, signs, things like that."

Beth questioned, "Will we know when the shopper will attend? It seems that people might get a little nervous or even defensive if they think they're being watched or judged."

"They're being watched and judged anyway," Jeff said. "The only difference is that we're not benefiting from the feedback. A church may want to get the board or leadership team to buy into the idea first, and they will have to make the decision of whether the staff is informed. Or you may want to just spring a secret shopper on everybody without warning. Every situation is different. At Family Church, I think that as long as a team of a half-dozen people are aware of what we're doing and why, that is sufficient. I suppose in congregations where there is rarely a visitor, an announced shopper program could ruin it."

"This is a small detail," said Gary, "but how does the shopper record feedback? Won't it be obvious if she has a clipboard and walks around writing down impressions?"

"That would be obvious," Jeff commented, "wouldn't it? The shopper will be instructed to act as a regular newcomer. We should specify when to arrive, how long to stay and what aspects of the ministry to experience. There will be plenty of opportunities to write down brief notes and comments during the service time. The shopper should write down as much as possible right after she leaves the church. Within the week, the shopper should provide a written synopsis of the experience and meet with the pastor and quality team members."

Gary scribbled down a flurry of notes and asked, "What should we expect in the report? Is the shopper supposed to tell us what we did wrong or how we could do better?"

"Each shopper is different," Jeff responded, "but the goal is a descriptive report of what the shopper saw, did and experienced. Remember, we're hiring new eyes to see things that we cannot see as a regular. We want to see how a newcomer feels and thinks. Most of us are not as good as we think, and some of us are better than we give ourselves credit for."

Beth's hand went up halfway as she questioned, "But what do we do with the information after we've gathered it? People can get pretty defensive when it comes to being 'shopped.'"

"The information should be respected," Jeff replied, "and used in such a way that it can benefit the church and individuals. If a ministry or person is critiqued negatively, you'll want to treat it like any other constructive feedback. Initially, you may want to talk to the person individually. You may want to discuss items with ministry directors. You may just want to keep it confidential for the time being. Every situation is different."

"But what if you get a shopper whose comments are so off-the-wall," Gary pleaded, "or so out of sync with you and your ministry situation that their observations seem irrelevant?"

"We should never dismiss any critique," Jeff answered. "Criticism is our most important resource for growth and improvement, even though it may sting a bit. If we do a good job selecting and training a solid, representative shopper, then we need to take the feedback seriously. To pass off the secret shopper feedback as trivial or irrelevant is dangerous. At the same time, you can also pinpoint items that may not mesh with our church philosophy. For example, if we were a contemporary church seeking pre-Christians, we might not seriously consider a comment asking where the pipe organ music was."

"It would seem that the secret shopper idea would work best if done periodically, so we could look for trends," Beth added.

"That's a good point," said Jeff. "Everyone has 'off' days. Over time, good and bad trends emerge. You can also measure improvements by having a secret shopper come in after you've made changes in a ministry."

Gary asked, "How often should we have a shopper come?"

"That all depends on how much unbiased feedback we are seeking," said Jeff. "I think that for a normal church, every three to six months is sufficient. We tend to go in spurts at Majesty Suites. We'll have a regular shopper quarterly, but if we're implementing a new service or program, we may bring in a secret shopper right away."

Beth suggested, "What about our phone manners? A lot of companies today inform you that your calls may be screened for quality assurance."

"It may not be a bad idea for a church as well," Jeff agreed. "I think just asking the shopper to call in once for information would be sufficient. We may want to make that a tag on to the visit report."

"Well," Gary's eyes widened with enthusiasm, "this secret shopper thing is a terrific idea! I'm excited to try it out, so go for it, Jeff. Let's get together after we've had our first secret shopper."

The way you see your future determines your thinking today, and your thinking today determines your performance today.

—TONY CAMPOLO

THE GIST OF IT...
WHY WE DO WHAT WE DO AND THE WAY WE DO IT

People today are consumer minded, meaning they are looking for congregations and ministries that meet their needs. Most pastors have noticed this change through the years. Although families used to be more loyal along denominational lines, a recent survey shows that most parishioners have a "Heinz 57" religious bloodline. People have always had some of the shopping mentality when seeking a place of worship, but today they are more up front about it.

"We're just church shopping right now," they say, as they shake your hand on the way out. In other words, *Don't try to sell me. I may or may not be back, based on how I like the church down the street.*

Is such thinking wrong? The answer is yes! Every time you have a visitor who lives within driving distance, you are being shopped. They are looking at your architecture, decor, rest rooms, classrooms and sanctuary. They are checking out the attire and friendliness of the people. They are taking mental notes as the music plays and the message is delivered.

Most people make their decision after one time whether or not they will return. If they like what they see and feel, they usually come back again. If they return a third time, there is a 90 percent chance they'll stay, at least for a while.

Because so many decisions are made on first impressions, we need to harvest feedback from those who shop us.

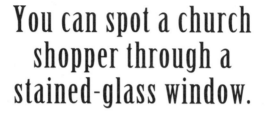

You can spot a church shopper through a stained-glass window.

Stan Toler and Mark Toler-Hollingsworth, *You Might Be a Preacher If...* Volume II (Tulsa, Okla.: Albury Press, 1997), p. 135. Used with permission.

The most obvious church-shopping experience is Sunday morning worship, but you may want to get feedback on adult, youth or children's classes—even a midweek service. Often pastors and ministry leaders take their cues from current users of the ministry instead of thinking how those who are not using the ministry are feeling. Certain people do not attend programs and events for various reasons. It could be marketing, or it could be because we are alienating them in some way.

The problem with this shopper program is that it can be intimidating, especially if a pastor or ministry receives a negative mark. The information will not be effective if it is never acted upon, or if it is hidden by those who did not receive high marks.

Think through how you want to use the secret-shopper information. A senior pastor or ministry director may want to use the information solely for his own benefit. The best way is a team approach to decide which information can honestly be discussed. For example, if the sermon gets dinged or the music receives a thumbs-down, that can create negative energy among the staff. Again, discretion is advised.

Any feedback from a secret shopper should be put into proper context. No one should get fired or lose his or her place with a ministry based on the feedback of a single shopper. Everyone experiences an "off" Sunday. Analyze the report, trying not to overreact to it.

The following is an overview of the main points necessary for implementing a secret-shopper program at your church:

1. Discuss the secret shopper idea with appropriate people. Help them understand the need for such a program. Request the finances to recruit and train a shopper.
2. Contact potential shoppers. The person being considered should not be a part of the church, but should understand the community demographics.
3. Provide training insights for the secret shopper. Have the shopper observe a normal Sunday, unless otherwise desired.
4. Ask the shopper to attend a church service.
5. Meet with the ministry team within a week of the visit to review written and verbal feedback of the shopper's experience.

6. Use the information to enhance ministries, instruct people and build the team. Avoid embarrassing people.

7. Follow up on all changes discussed and implemented. You may want to schedule a follow-up visit from your shopper at a later date. (For more detailed report ideas, see appendix A.)

QUESTIONS AND ANSWERS

Q. In my church, I'm afraid it could offend people if they found out we had a secret shopper. They might think I don't trust them, that I don't think we're doing a good enough job.

Alan: The secret shopper is a stand-alone idea, but it obviously works best in a quality-improvement environment. When people are thinking improvement, customer service and ministry excellence, then the idea of having an anonymous party check us out makes a lot of sense.

Most progressive businesspeople are familiar with the concept and will likely applaud a church for being willing to take a look at itself objectively. The fear of offending people can be addressed individually from church to church. If your congregation might not be ready for a secret shopper, maybe a quiet individual or team-oriented feedback would be sufficient. The bottom line is that people are shopping your church all the time. The goal is to find out what they are thinking, feeling and perceiving.

Stan: Churches shouldn't be afraid of being critiqued. In Philippians 4:9, Paul writes: "Put into practice what you learned from me, what you heard and saw and realized. Do that, and God, who makes everything work together, will work you into his most excellent harmonies" (*The Message*).

With all due respect to Robert Schuller and Dale Galloway, I would like to propose the Five-Star Church Achiever's Creed: "What the Five-Star Church can conceive, whatever it dares to believe, with God's help it can achieve." Yes, emphatically so, I think we should come under the magnifying glass of the secret church shopper.

Q. As a pastor, I am a little unsure of what our people will say if the shopper's report critiques me negatively. I've taken some shots in recent months, and I'm not sure if I want to be vulnerable anymore.

Stan: Criticism has always been a challenge for pastors. Yet if you observe the sports world today, the teams that achieve excellence give and receive feedback. I recommend the following steps:

1. Listen and learn.
2. Resolve concerns.
3. Ask for a commitment to grow.
4. Establish the process.

The road to the next level is always uphill.
—TALMADGE JOHNSON

Q. Honestly, where am I going to get a secret shopper? I can't imagine asking someone to come "shop" our church. A complete stranger would think I'm nuts, and a friend might be biased.

Alan: If you approach this as a professional service, where you are willing to train and pay a person to come experience your church for the purpose of feedback, you should not lack for interest.

If your goal is to get feedback from other churched people, your options are even easier. You can talk to a sister congregation nearby or a similar-style church not far away. If your goal is to reach the unchurched, you can find neighbors, work associates, local clerks, merchants or parent-teacher organization members to contact. Begin with the profile and look for people who reflect those characteristics.

Stan: I would recommend finding a friendly greeter at a local Wal-Mart store and inviting him to come to the church as the secret shopper. Sam Walton knew how to train his "associates," as he called them.

*Team leaders know how to accept
praise and criticism.*

—STAN TOLER

YOU MIGHT BE A PREACHER IF...

You'd like to recruit some of Wal-Mart's greeters.

Stan Toler and Mark Toler-Hollingsworth, *You Might Be a Preacher If...* Volume II (Tulsa, Okla.: Albury Press, 1997), p. 113. Used with permission.

It's not what you are going to do, but it's what you are doing now that counts.

—NAPOLEON HILL

THE DOERS SECTION

- How do we feel about hiring a secret shopper to come and "shop" our church?
- How will this work in our ministry context?
- Who would be good to serve on the shopper advisory team?
- What kind of a shopper should we recruit?
- Who specifically will be responsible for recruiting and debriefing the shopper?
- In what areas do we want the shopper to review our church? (See appendix A for ideas.)
- When will this be accomplished?
- What will we do with the feedback we receive?

Celebrate what you want to see more of.

—TOM PETERS

Evaluation and Measurement

★ ★ ★ ★ ★

*If you don't know where you're going, you're likely
to end up someplace else.*

—YOGI BERRA

"So Beth, did you find a secret shopper last week?" asked Jeff.

"It was incredible," said Beth. "Finding someone was much easier than I thought. She was a nice lady with two kids and she 'shopped' us last Sunday. Yesterday I was debriefed about her visit. Her feedback was very helpful. We learned several things about what we're doing well and what we need to do better, especially when people visit Family Church for the first time. Her comments, for the most part, seemed in-line with my thoughts, but a few things she noticed surprised me."

Gary squeaked, "I'm afraid to find out what she said about my message."

"And if I want to keep my job, I don't think I'll share that with you, either," Beth laughed. "Just kidding; her report was very positive."

"Whew," Gary sighed, "this quality-improvement stuff is fine, as long as I don't have to change anything."

Jeff nodded in agreement, "You wouldn't believe how often I have to eat crow here at Majesty Suites when an idea I come up with gets bombed by a thoughtful critique."

"It takes a strong ego to pursue this feedback," Gary replied.

Beth asked, "So, how do we avoid getting people upset about subjective feedback that may be argued from both sides?"

"Evaluation and quantification are essential," said Jeff. "Otherwise, it becomes personal."

"But you see, we're in the faith business," Gary replied. "We help people spiritually grow. How in the world do you quantify that?"

"Good point," said Jeff, smiling, "but we still need to measure aspects of our service to see how we're doing. By gathering this information, our staff meetings can become less defensive because it's tough to argue with third-person feedback and documented measurements."

"That's going to be a shift for any church," Gary said. "Surveys and measurements seem so intimidating and even irreligious."

"Think of it in terms of fruit inspecting," replied Jeff. "Jesus said, 'By their fruit you will know them.' We have a lot of measurable items in the Bible, like how long Creation took, how long it rained on Noah and the ark, how many disciples Jesus had, and how many people he fed with the loaves and fishes."

"Our worship folder says, 'We count people because people count' by the weekly attendance figures," said Beth.

"I once had a professor who said, 'If it's real, you can measure it,'" said Jeff. "The challenge is to figure out what we want to measure and the best way to gain reliable data."

"Okay," Gary said, taking the bait, "what are some ideas we can use to measure quality at Family Church?"

"Well, let's start with the obvious," said Jeff. "We need to look at attendance and financial trends. What I've seen from most churches is that they over- or underestimate the importance of tracking these two factors. People will give more when they are excited about what is happening. Flat or declining numbers in any ministry should be indicators to check further."

"We're not just a business," Beth added, "focused on numbers. How do we avoid all this becoming a numbers game?"

"I'm involved in a business, but I don't prioritize numbers," said Jeff. "By emphasizing good service at Majesty Suites, we believe the numbers will follow."

Gary noted, "But it seems that you can do something well, really well, and the numbers won't reflect the level of quality."

"True, very true," Jeff conceded. "Let me pick on you in the church a little. For example, I know that we have people at Family Church who enjoy pipe organ music. If we built the finest pipe organ and hired the best musician to play it, would that make more people come to our church in droves? Probably not. In other words, we're doing something with excellence, but that in and of itself is not our goal. Our ministry objective is to reach people. Unfortunately, there is not a large group of people interested in pipe-organ music."

Beth asked, "So where do you draw the line? Do you throw a wild party with free beer because you know a certain number of people will be attracted to that? If people think Majesty Suites is too expensive, do you cut your prices in half just to fill the rooms?"

"Every organization," Jeff elaborated, "every business, must ask itself the questions: Why are we in business? Why do we exist? If the church's business is to provide organ music, since we're using that for an illustration, then we should never deviate from that value. If we're in business to effectively communicate the gospel with people who are not in the church, then we'd better do whatever it takes to reach them, so long as it does not break a spiritual principle. From what I read in the Bible, style of music is not the issue. The attitude with which we sing is. Regarding lowering our rates at Majesty Suites, we could do that so long as we could turn a profit. If we did not turn a profit for long, we would be out of business."

"So you admit that you're in the money-making business." Beth stated.

"Of course we are," said Jeff, "but we are also in the customer-service business. If we make money, but don't serve customers well, we are just as much going against our core values as if we don't make money. It's not an either/or situation. It's a both/and scenario. The bottom line is that if you do not raise enough money at Family Church, you won't be able to help people. You'll have to lay off staff, turn off the lights, and close the doors."

"This is a very interesting discussion," said Gary. "Okay, we're sold on the importance of measuring ministry effectiveness. What other means of measurement are there beyond obvious attendance and offerings?"

"Well, one tool for measuring follow-up that we use at Majesty Suites is pressure-sensitive copy forms. We found that feedback was falling through the cracks. We developed a form that allows us to route different forms to the various departments."

Jeff passed out a sample to Gary and Beth.

"I love it," said Beth. "It looks like a good tool."

"We could adapt this survey for first-time visitors," said Jeff. "When a person visits Majesty Suites for the first time, we give them a simple survey to fill out that has a stamp already on it for mailing."

Beth asked, "Do people really fill these out?"

"If you give them an incentive, they do," said Jeff. "We give them a discount coupon if they drop it off at the front desk or mail the survey to us. You have to make it worth their while."

Gary nodded. "We could offer a gift of some sort that would motivate our visitors to respond on the communication cards and return a survey."

"Sure, we could," said Jeff. "The survey should be brief. It should take a minute or two to complete. Ten or fifteen questions would be the optimum. A few open-ended questions at the end can elicit a longer response."

Beth examined the form and inquired, "How do you use these survey results from visitors?"

"We look for trends," Jeff pointed out. "If a few people begin commenting on the food quality in Capers, saying it's not good, then we meet with the staff and brainstorm. We'll often send copies to various departments. Allowing the staff to see feedback regarding their area of responsibility helps them to take ownership. Another way to get feedback is to provide suggestion boxes. This provides for anonymity."

Beth was curious. "What do you do with off-the-wall comments?"

"Again, we look for trends," said Jeff. "Naturally, in a church you're not going to please everyone, just as we don't at Majesty Suites. But it would help a lot if you could find out whether the person fits the profile of someone you're trying to target. If not, you can hear their comments, but not necessarily weigh them the same as a person who represents a group you're trying to reach."

"You mentioned that you periodically survey customers," Beth replied. "How often do you do this?"

"Once or twice a year we'll survey our regular customers to see how we're doing," said Jeff. "You can't ask too many questions, but you can target certain areas of service. On a quarterly basis in the church, you could do a worship-folder survey highlighting certain areas of ministry that you want to assess. Allow some open-ended questions for people to give miscellaneous feedback. Tabulate the results into a single document and have the ministry directors and supervision team read the results. Another thing you could do is hire a third party to conduct brief phone interviews. You can pick out names to receive the calls, selecting those you want to get feedback from in an area of ministry that they use."

"I suppose that the feedback is tabulated and turned in again for staff review," said Gary.

"Sure, it is," Jeff acknowledged. "This is basically a low-budget approach to marketing research that goes on constantly in large corporations. A more elaborate vehicle is focus groups, where you invite a group of people who are current or potential church members, and provide a place for four to eight people to provide face-to-face comments. You can learn a lot around a dessert table in someone's home. The focus groups may be in conjunction with the potential launch of a new service or ministry, or it can be simply to discuss how various ministry consumers are perceiving the church. You don't want to get a bunch of 'yes' people, just as you don't want a group of negative people. You may want to train a third party to ask the questions, or you may want to divide the workload among a few leaders or ministry directors."

Gary asked, "How do you quantify this feedback?"

"Good question," Jeff replied, as he warmed to the subject. "The goal would be to have a somewhat unbiased report that provided written information that others could read and respond to. I think that a survey could be added to the focus groups, or you could just record main points and ideas for others to see."

Gary had an idea. "Why couldn't we, at the end of a class, seminar or workshop, automatically pass out feedback sheets that members could fill out and turn in anonymously?"

"I like that," said Jeff. "In the example of an adult class, we could ask two or three questions about the teacher and his effectiveness, two or three questions on the lesson, and maybe a few questions about things like sound, seating, length, etc. If we begin creating a quality-improvement culture, people will get used to this. One more feedback tool that most churches and even most businesses overlook is the exit interview. Have we ever had anyone leave Family Church?"

Gary and Beth laughed nervously.

"Ah," Gary said, trying to look serious, "I think there was one family, three or four years ago, who moved out of state."

Jeff explained, "Whenever someone who has been active gets up and leaves, you have an excellent opportunity to find out why. The reasons may be theological, stylistic, personal or something else. The bottom line is that you need to know. If the pastoral staff doesn't gather the information, then get someone who will. Get the facts. Avoid the rumors that abound when people leave. This will help you know how to avoid losing people who might have been offended by a staff member, or who did not feel their child was receiving quality care, or who were tired of fighting for a parking place, or who did not relate to the style of worship music."

"We've done that informally from time to time," Gary noted, "but we could really do that more consistently."

"Who knows," Beth added, "our interest may even bring people back who left with just a single bad experience."

"I know I keep coming back to the same old concern," Gary sighed, "but these are volunteers we're talking about for the most part. How can you put these people, who are donating their time, under the magnifying glass that allows others to critique their service?"

"The difference," said Jeff, "as I see it, is that in a loving attitude you'll need to explain why we invite constructive criticism. If the goal is people growth and ministry improvement, help them understand how this feedback can enhance their ministry. These comments may also overlap into what they do in the marketplace and augment their professional skills as well."

"I think it could work," Beth stated. "I think most people would rise to the task."

"Agreed!" Jeff exclaimed. "We're around excellence all week, and then we come to church and let down our standards for some reason."

Gary nodded. "It goes back to the fundamental premise we talked about first: God deserves our best."

People judge churches the same way
they judge restaurants.

—TOM McCASLIN

THE GIST OF IT...
WHY WE DO WHAT WE DO AND THE WAY WE DO IT

Quality-oriented organizations frequently seek information that can give them objective feedback as to how they are doing. With a growing number of organizations being service oriented versus product oriented, a growing number of tools and instruments allows us to measure our service quality. Churches, for the most part, have not tapped into this concept. We need to develop our own instruments.

The first question to ask is: Why are we afraid? Don't pass this off lightly. We often avoid measuring our ministries because we're afraid to find out what people *really* think. No one enjoys learning that changes may be necessary. We like to think we're okay just the way we are. The emperor who had no clothes deluded himself into believing that everything was all right. No one spoke up until the young child pointed out that the emperor was, indeed, naked. Surveys and feedback measurements have a way of pulling back the covers.

Some might think that surveys fall short, in that you end up trying to give what people want. Since our goal is to start with the truth of Christ and reach people, we must have a consumer-oriented mind-set that will help us develop methods that will allow us to communicate the message more effectively. The eternal truths of Christ are unchanging. The styles and methods of worship tend to be cultural, meaning they change over time. A church service in New Guinea is different from one in Scottsdale, Arizona. One is not necessarily better, but they *should* differ, according to the culture. The important thing is worshiping God and teaching His ways.

Information is our friend. Gather it. Make sure it has validity. Surveying a few happy followers will hardly represent a proper perspective of a church or ministry. Include the happy few, but go beyond them. Seek feedback from visitors, neighbors and regulars. Use all sorts of measuring instruments so that you do not rely on a single, one-page, annual survey that states: "How are we doing? Give us your ministry ideas." Providing regular feedback channels allows us to track ministry quality long term. When quality quirks arise, we can begin to recognize trends and target problem people or areas.

When feedback gathering is too sporadic, we can miss key feedback to make a ministry better. Rarely is everything all right and all wrong on any given day. We want to see patterns for the most part, but sometimes, specifics help us see the big-picture trends. As we improve the big picture, the details will begin to take care of themselves.

The following 10 examples of feedback instruments can provide qualitative and quantitative information as to how a ministry is doing. There is an old adage: "Statistics never lie, but liars use statistics." That can hold true here, if the ways you develop these instruments do not reflect the true health of a ministry. Putting in the energy first will help you alleviate the frustration of unclear and conflicting feedback. Having said that, don't be intimidated to get started. There are many simple ways to harvest feedback on ministry health beyond the subjective, How do you think it's going?

Finally, you can provide answers to surveys that are numerically oriented. For example, you can ask people to circle the appropriate number to a question such as, Did the teacher keep your interest by providing adequate visual aids and handouts? The numerical responses available would be as follows:

1. Not at all
2. Could have been better
3. Good
4. Very Good
5. Excellent

In this way, you can compare averages in various categories and then compare classes, teachers and materials over time. The goal is to improve ministry effectiveness.

1. MINISTRIES, CHURCH ATTENDANCE AND FINANCES
Questions to ask:

Are we growing?
How does our monthly average this year compare with the monthly average last year? The last five years?

What are the trends?

How are the individual services, programs and ministries doing in attendance?

Do we track small groups and Sunday School classes to see what percentage of our regular attendees are in a smaller group environment?

How do the finances compare now as previously?

How many new regular givers have emerged?

What is the average gift amount?

Is there a campaign that has skewed these numbers? Providing line charts, bar charts and graphs can add much to the visual presentation of these statistics. These statistics will often not provide the information to explain the trends, but information from other measuring instruments can often do this. The goal is not to get overly concerned with short-term changes, as much as trends. If you always do what you've always done, you'll always get what you've always gotten. To think otherwise is wrongheaded.

2. FIRST-TIME ATTENDEES AND GUESTS

First impressions are lasting, meaningful ones. You can't ask a regular attendee to give you a feel of how things are and assume that it is valid. We all see things differently in the beginning than after being involved awhile. All a newcomer has to go on are his first impressions. If this works against you, your church and ministry will not have much growth because guests will not come back. As mentioned in the previous chapter, some studies show that after a person has visited for the third time, there is a 90 percent chance that person will remain for some length of time. Therefore, those early impressions are vital for continued growth.

The questions we need to ask are:

What feedback do we want to gather from visitors?

How will we get them to fill out forms or respond to surveys?

How can we get them to leave their names and addresses to
follow up with such a request?

Traditional methods, such as having guests stand up during
the service, signifying them with a visitor's badge or rose, or asking
them to sign a guest book as they enter the church, all tend to be
threatening in today's church environment. Therefore, we must
appear to be detached and reserved in our approach, while making
it worth their while to give us their time and energy.

Providing incentive gifts is one very helpful way. Why not offer
the "Jesus" video to first-time guests filling out a communication
card, or a free magazine or restaurant certificate for second-time
attendees, or a book or music CD for third-time guests? Such an
incentive program helps you track newcomers better to allow for
more adequate follow-up. All the while, you avoid appearing to corner
them or make them stand out, something most of us hate.

Use newcomer feedback to learn how people found out about
the church, one thing they really liked, or one idea to make your
church even better. A short, simple feedback card (self-addressed
and postage-paid) makes feedback gathering nonthreatening.

3. QUARTERLY SURVEYS TARGETING CERTAIN MINISTRIES

A quarterly church feedback survey that takes less than 60 seconds
to complete is not too much to ask. You can include it in a Sunday
morning worship folder and even take time during announcements
to mention it. If you mail them out, don't plan on receiving many
back, even if you provide a self-addressed, stamped envelope.

Churches with Web sites can provide the survey on-line, or
churches without Web sites can e-mail it to e-mail addresses. This
new technology tends to elicit higher responses. You can't really
survey the entire church via a simple survey, so you might want to
target two to three ministries or areas, specifically. Of course, provide one or two open-ended questions to let the respondents voice
their opinions.

Some items might include: nursery, hospitality (greeters, ushers, information finding), small groups, pastoral care, service elements, youth and Sunday School. A simple, two-sided sheet titled "How Are We Doing?" with 5 to 10 questions with names optional can be used. Churches with strong small groups and Sunday School structures may be more effective at doing this, except that you will miss feedback from those not in these ministries.

By providing anonymity, you encourage people to be honest and open. However, all feedback is not created equal. More weight should be given to those within your target ministry group than those outside the prime-target group. Anonymous surveys do not provide this, but they can give you a sense of trends that a face-to-face interview might not provide.

4. THIRD-PARTY INTERVIEWS

If at all possible, conduct phone or face-to-face interviews. This feedback is more thorough than a survey and, if deemed important, certain areas can be probed more deeply. If you use someone from outside the church to conduct the interview, you communicate your willingness to look objectively at your ministry.

Someone from your church needs to give an orientation to the interviewer. An option is to have board members or lay leaders conduct these interviews instead of the pastoral staff, who are probably too busy.

Debriefing with the interviewer is important, and written feedback is important to keep on file as well. Just as important as *what* is asked is *who* is asked. Select a pool of people from whom you want certain information and then let the interviewer determine those to be interviewed. If you provide a larger group of names, you can have the interviewer gather information such as age, duration in church, etc.

5. END OF CLASS, WORKSHOP, SERIES FEEDBACK SHEETS

A quality-improvement process means actively harvesting feedback on teachers, programs, events and curriculum. Many seminar businesses provide a feedback sheet for participants as a regular part of the seminar, which helps them review the participants' sense of satisfaction. Although this may seem intimidating for the teacher or event leader, the feedback will improve future lessons and events. A one-page survey can be passed out to class members after a workshop series that asks them to respond to items such as room setup, lighting, location, lesson content, teacher clarity, effectiveness in communicating and other parts of the course experience.

The results can be reviewed by the teacher and the ministry director. If the group is too large to ask everyone to respond to a survey, you can randomly pick a few to fill out a feedback sheet, trusting that the sample represents the larger group. Questionnaires that provide specific issues and a couple of open-ended questions help ministry leaders avoid asking questions such as "Did you enjoy the class?"

6. FOCUS GROUPS

Gathering a group of people to discuss ministry issues face-to-face allows for greater depth and exploration to take place than written surveys and questionnaires. You may use a focus group to brain-storm on new projects or test-market a ministry or church event before you implement it. A focus group that represents your church or a certain social group within your church can give you invalu-able information as to how people are thinking and feeling.

Focus groups happen all the time, whether we realize it or not. They take place in church lobbies, in restaurants and at home Bible studies. People talk. They share their joys, frustrations, opinions and ideas. By intentionally gathering a group, you focus the atten-tion on a specific ministry or topic, and you can record these thoughts. Focus groups can also result in better understanding among group attendees. The goal of a typical focus group is not to persuade people to think a certain way, but it is designed for lead-ers to find clarity for church ministry.

Focus groups can be led by ministry leaders or neutral facilitators inside or outside a congregation. Carefully select a focus group leader who has good listening skills, who asks penetrating questions, and who can handle potential conflict without becoming defensive. A good group leader can engage in a conversation without becoming emotionally engaged himself.

Emotional and spiritual maturity and congregational commitment are assets for an in-house focus group leader. Notes from the groups can be presented to the appropriate ministry leaders, and surveys can be used to solicit ideas and stimulate group discussion.

7. SUGGESTION BOXES

There is nothing new or fancy about this old-fashioned system for gathering information. Still, people like to share their ideas. Encourage them to applaud something done well or share an idea on how things can be done better. Providing a box where anonymous comments can be made—as they occur, where they occur—communicates that important feedback to the church. Obviously, it is helpful to keep the box equipped with paper, pencils and pens.

Every church is different. Congregations that are in portable facilities will find this practice difficult. Portable suggestion boxes, note cards or clipboards might suffice. It is important to periodically remind team members to encourage ministry customers to share their ideas. Sometimes people share their ideas during busy times of ministry, which diverts care and attention away from others. When a suggestion box is nearby, the staff member can suggest that the person write down the idea so that "we can give it the quality attention it deserves, since we are busy trying to serve others right now."

8. EXIT INTERVIEWS

Some of the most valuable information for ministry improvement is lost when we do not ask people why they left the church. Naturally, you can't follow up with every person, and in some cases, you already know why that family is leaving.

The people you want to pursue are those who seem to fit your target group. Once a person is MIA (missing in action), contact can be made in the context of wondering why the person was active and then inactive. Ironically, you'll find that some people will return to church because they sense that someone cared, that they were missed, and maybe just needed a little loving nudge. Others can benefit from having a situation explained or rectified.

Therefore, the contact, whether over the phone or in written form, needs to be nonthreatening and with an attitude that says, "We really want to do better in serving people. Could you please help by telling us why you did not find the ministry of our church fulfilling enough to stay?"

Naturally, there is a window of time in which an exit interview should be conducted. Anything less than a month is too soon.

The survey or interview should ask questions such as:

- How long did you attend our church?
- Have you found another church home?
- What do you like best about your new church?
- Would you cite a specific reason why you left our church?

Questions such as these help uncover potential motivations for leaving. Remember: You can't be all things to all people. The information you glean from people within your target ministry group is worth a lot more than information from those outside the group.

Exit interviews can also help disarm people who have had a negative experience and did not feel that anyone cared. Studies show that people who have a good experience will tell one to three others. When people have a bad experience, they tell 7 to 12 other people. Exit interviews can help diminish the amount of negative advertising that goes on among those who have had a negative experience. By communicating concern and even apologizing, if necessary, you may not be able to reclaim a former attendee, but you can avoid a stream of negative publicity from offended former attendees.

Those doing the exit interviews should be mature, committed church members who will not be overly influenced by comments or perceptions of those who left. If you have an interviewer agreeing that the pastor is a jerk or the service really is shoddy, then you may lose more than the interviewee in the process. If nothing else, it gives your church one more time to say, "Thanks for giving us the opportunity to minister to you for the time you were here. We'll pray for you as you seek another church home."

9. COMMUNITY SURVEY

An interesting tool for some churches is putting together a community survey. This could mean hiring a marketing firm or making it a project for a local college marketing class. Churches that seek to change their images within a community might find the going tough if there is a negative perception of them in their neighborhoods.

Long-term congregations should invest the time and resources to monitor community perceptions. Many congregations become frustrated with their lack of growth following a new pastor or building addition. These congregations do not understand that little has been done to change a less-than-positive perception of their church within the community. Worse yet, they assume that the community knew that things had changed.

This concept helps explain why multiple restaurants can open and close in the same location. Each restaurant thinks theirs will be different, but community perception often keeps people from giving a new restaurant another try. Prior to investing money and energy into a community outreach campaign, a church should know what perceptions exist in the community.

The goal is to determine whether the perception is negative or positive, and how strongly that perception is. All of this will help in determining what needs to be done prior to making perception changes. You will waste money and energy in striving to change community perceptions if you do not invest time and energy beforehand to see specifically what needs to be changed.

Gathering before-and-after data can also help you determine the success of a perception campaign, which is good stewardship. To throw resources into a community outreach program without measuring results is poor stewardship. Was the money well spent? How do you know unless you measure results.

10. COMBINED RESEARCH

The most effective feedback instrument is a combination of ideas presented in this chapter. Every church should brainstorm and experiment with varying measurement tools. Because so few congregations seriously take an organized approach to quality improvement, a large number of instruments like these, modified for church use, do not exist.

Hopefully, we will see more congregations developing, testing and sharing their findings so that others can modify them for their use. The old idea of not sharing ideas and tools will not work in the twenty-first century. When the quality of other churches is raised, so is ours, and we will enhance the Kingdom.

Most of us know the adverse results of being associated with negative church experiences such as legalism, moral failure or televangelist scandals. These experiences lower the positive perceptions people have about church and make working in the ministry more difficult. A strong emphasis on quality improvement, however, will raise this perception and make it easier for each one of us to attract and retain people for effective use in the Kingdom.

To improve is to change; to be perfect is to change often.

—WINSTON CHURCHILL

QUESTIONS AND ANSWERS

Q. Surveys, questionnaires, phone interviews and focus groups all seem pretty invasive. I'm not sure our people will respond

positively to this approach to ministry improvement. How can I sell the concept to our people?

Alan: As we've been saying from the start, without a quality-improvement mind-set, many of these ideas will seem out of place and threatening. Within a quality-improvement structure, they make sense. Feedback gathering will become a natural part of how you conduct ministry at your church. A little explanation can go a long way.

People may want to know the motivation behind the survey. Congregations not used to surveys can confuse a survey with a vote. A survey merely measures opinions. A vote means a majority usually wins approval of a new idea or change. A survey can also create anxiety by implying something may be wrong, so you need to create a context in which feedback gathering is normal. Another way to explain it is that you're merely trying to receive opinions and ideas that can only help the church.

Stan: Not long ago I was in Knoxville, Tennessee, and I dined at the Chop House restaurant. While waiting to be seated, I had an opportunity to read their values statement. One statement struck me profoundly. It said, "At Chop House we are guest-obsessed. We will go to any extreme to please the customer." Wow!

My dining experience at Chop House was awesome. After the meal, I was asked to evaluate my dining experience through filling out a Guest Survey Card. I gave them five stars!

Personally, I think people today are getting used to surveys and polls. Therefore, pastors using positive communication techniques can and will find support for such instruments.

Q. I'm so busy. Is it realistic to think of measuring ministry performance? Seems like one more thing to do in a busy schedule.

Stan: I heard NBA basketball coach Pat Riley say, "Complacency is the last hurdle any winner, any team, must overcome before attaining potential greatness." Regardless of how busy pastors might be, it behooves them to use instruments of evaluation. These learning experiences can be used to shake churches out of a lethargic, complacent state!

The only people who like change in your church are the wet babies.

Stan Toler and Mark Toler-Hollingsworth, *You Might Be a Preacher If...* Volume II (Tulsa, Okla.: Albury Press, 1997), p. 77. Used with permission.

Alan: I'm reminded of the story about the lumberjack who was known for his great chopping skills. When someone asked him his secret, he said, "I always take time to sharpen the ax."

Of course, while he's sharpening his ax, he's not chopping, but he knows that chopping with a sharp ax will make his job easier than using a dull ax. Taking the time to survey and measure ministry effectiveness is like sharpening the ax. Do not confuse ministry activity and busyness with effectiveness.

By improving ministry, we can often avoid the cleanup necessary with sloppy and mediocre ministry. That ultimate goal is to decrease our workload and improve fruitfulness by implementing new ideas and improve service. Find time to develop quality-measuring instruments, implement them, and then use the feedback appropriately.

Q. What if you receive feedback on a ministry or person who is unwilling to change?

Alan: Another way to ask that is: What if the feedback says that the pastor's messages are dry and perplexing? Can we send him to a preaching seminar or motivate him to enroll in Toastmasters?

If not, then we should probably not push him. We need to know what we can and cannot change. If we do not have the money for an entire new facility, do we have the resources to paint and renovate it? What the feedback gives us is information to know what we need to do. Subsequent discussions tell us how much we need to pursue the changes and whether or not we can solve the issues.

Being able to fix all situations is unlikely. When we come to a situation where change is unlikely, we must ask the bigger question: How much is this hurting our ministry? It may mean eventually finding a new staff member. It may mean relocating the church. It may mean letting a ministry or congregation die. These are the tough issues requiring prayer, wisdom and loving discussion.

Stan: Someone once said, "That which holds one's attention determines one's actions." If we give our attention to important matters, our goal of good decision making will be achieved. I'm with Alan on the boring sermons. There's no excuse for boring sermons. So here we go with a Top Ten Countdown:

TOP TEN THINGS PARISHIONERS DO
WHEN THE SERMON IS BORING

10. Crack their knuckles.
9. Eat a box of Tic-Tacs.
8. Clip their fingernails.
7. Clean out their purses.
6. Smile insincerely.
5. Slap their sleeping neighbors to see if they'll turn the other cheek.
4. Make out grocery lists on the back of tithe envelopes.
3. Pass notes.
2. Play Hangman.
1. Sleep!

Q. How do we avoid becoming slaves to feedback and playing the numbers game?

Stan: We do that by focusing on people and building relationships. In my 30 years of pastoral service, I have seen the numbers mania come and go. Mostly go! Rock-solid church leadership should take good data and utilize it in terms of meeting the needs of parishioners.

Alan: People who play the numbers game tend to overemphasize a few statistics like the Sunday morning worship attendance and offering. As we mentioned, these are just two of a number of valuable measurements. Don't dismiss their importance, but expand your measurements to glean a better perspective on ministry health.

Your goal is not numbers; it is ministry excellence. If you pursue true excellence, the numbers will take care of themselves. Measuring our ministry effectiveness is a way of finding out whether we are helping transform the lives of people via our ministries. Measuring must be a vehicle, not the end goal. When you can provide statistical support for ministry improvement, it becomes more difficult for people involved in the process to argue against it.

A leader by definition is an innovator.

— WARREN BENNIS

THE DOERS SECTION

- What measuring do we do now? How could we use this information for quality improvements?
- What are the pros and cons of using measuring tools for ministry improvement?
- Why do churches tend to shy away from actively seeking measurable feedback?
- Which of the measuring instruments mentioned could we implement in our church?
- What specific plan do we have to carry out a survey or questionnaire?

    1. Who will develop the survey?
    2. What will it measure?
    3. When will it be implemented?
    4. Who will direct the flow of information?
    5. Who will we ask to respond?
    6. What will we do with it once it is gathered?

- Starting with the measurable information we now have available to us, what can we learn about the respective ministries?
- Discuss what you have learned about the ministry effectiveness.
- What are the implications of our discoveries?
- What can we do to improve?
- What other ministry-measuring ideas should we use that are not specifically mentioned in this chapter?

Chapter

9

Sweat the Small Stuff

★ ★ ★ ★ ★

ATTENTION TO DETAIL, EFFICIENCY AND EFFECTIVENESS

*Most churches today are caught up in religious
activity with very little accomplished.*

— STAN TOLER

The three quality-improvement team members of Family Church decided to travel to a mountaintop retreat center to hash out the remaining quality-improvement issues.

"Jeff, I appreciate you taking two days to help us wrap up this training time," Gary began. "I think a setting like this helps us focus better on what we need to do."

"Actually, it was Beth's idea to book Camp Pinerock," said Jeff. "Up here, we can work without any cell phones, beepers or interruptions."

"Any excuse to get away to pine trees and mountains is good enough for me," said Beth. "Why don't we pray and get started?"

The three entered a season of prayer, as they had done at the beginning of each previous session, seeking God's guidance as they sought to improve their ministry at Family Church. They realized much was at stake in these meetings. Current Family Church members, as well as people they had never met, depended on their ability to improve the church.

"Amen," said Gary, as their prayer time closed.

"Well," Jeff replied, "I have to admit that I've been thoroughly impressed with the two of you and how you've responded to many of these ideas. I spend most of my time working with people who eat and sleep quality-management issues. I have to admit that I was nervous discussing these issues with you, but you've responded well. I've seen great strides in our church, and it's because of your great attitudes."

"You know, while we're backslapping," said Gary, "I should tell you how impressed I've been with your willingness to teach us principles that have made Majesty Suites a five-star hotel. When we first laughed about the idea of having a five-star church, I figured that many of the principles you apply in the corporate world wouldn't fit the church world—that we were somehow more spiritual. That hasn't been the case. In fact, I'm a bit embarrassed that we didn't take quality-improvement issues more seriously before."

"Me too," Beth chimed in. "Having a background in business, I separated the two—church and business. I feel ashamed. I proudly looked down at businesses that promoted quality-improvement ideas, believing they were secular and pagan. I'm thinking that if we in the Church could glean some of the things that make profit-oriented organizations so effective, we could expand God's kingdom and bring Him glory in the process."

"Nice speech, Beth," Jeff exclaimed. "You've got it!"

Gary asked, "Got what?"

"Beth has caught the excellence mind-set," Jeff grinned, "a way of thinking that prevails among quality-oriented people. People can talk about quality issues from an intellectual standpoint but still not catch the way of thinking that goes along with true excellence. You and Beth have been different."

Gary responded, "Can we go home now?"

"No way," Beth jumped in. "I'm staying up here in the mountains, at least for the day."

"I said you had the mind-set," Jeff said, "not all the details, however. Our goal for the retreat is to go over the basic areas of quality that we want to consider. Developing a quality-improvement mind-set is not only important for everyone, but it's essential for your leadership team and ministry directors. At the same time, we need to do something more, and by that, I mean attention to detail."

"So you're saying that we need to sweat the small stuff," replied Gary.

"I am," said Jeff softly. "Our attention to detail must result in major and minor actions."

Gary sat back in his chair and sighed, "I keep getting this feeling that to be truly excellence oriented is a ton of work."

"At times it is," said Jeff. "The work that goes into improving a service or product from 90 to 97 percent can often require 20 to 40 percent *more* work. Obviously, we can't do everything with top-notch excellence. That would be poor stewardship. The best quality people know what needs to be the best and what can slide. Unfortunately, many businesses and ministries let far too much slide. Their inattention to detail results in mediocre facilities and programs."

Beth asked, "How do you get a feel of what is important?"

"Sounds like a wheat-and-chaff parable to me," said Pastor Gary.

"Well," Jeff smiled, "sweating the small stuff means taking care of the details that create a sense of excellence for the people involved in the ministry, both givers and receivers. People notice it."

"When you talk about detail," said Beth, "I imagine the foyer of Majesty Suites and the emphasis given to even the smallest requests of your guests. At Family Church, we're in the soul-growing business. What areas do we need to be concerned with in terms of details?"

"This is a good time to introduce the three main areas that need attention to detail in our church," said Jeff. "But when we talk about details, sometimes we lose our perspective on effectiveness."

"Run that by me again," Gary interrupted. "I'm not tracking."

"I'm probably not explaining it well," said Jeff. "Let me try it this way. McDonald's restaurants can make hamburgers efficiently and serve them with a smile. But if the burgers taste horrible, they won't sell any. In other words, McDonald's can prepare and nicely wrap a hamburger but the chain won't be effective if people don't eat the food. The lesson for us is that we run the risk of overlooking the bigger questions. In short, are we being effective?"

"This is interesting," said Beth.

"But you know another thing," Jeff continued, "I recently read a study showing that less than 15 percent of churches account for over half the people attending church on any given Sunday. These churches are effective, and they are quality oriented. Remember, quality will not guarantee effectiveness, but you'll rarely be effective without it."

"Wow," Gary's eyes lit up. "That statistic about one in seven churches accounting for over half of church attendance is amazing."

"And the percentage of people is growing," said Jeff.

"So," Gary questioned, "are they quality because they have growing congregations, or are they growing because they have quality, Jeff?"

"Quality, like everything in life, tends to beget itself. What you find is that people and resources are attracted to excellence, which allows you to increase quality even more."

"It's like physics," Beth said. "A body in motion tends to remain in motion, and a body at rest tends to remain at rest. Success tends to perpetuate itself, and ineffectiveness tends to maintain itself."

"Nicely said, Beth," Jeff applauded, "but that's where leadership comes into play. A leader's job is to catalyze change and help organizations become more effective. The manager's job is to pursue efficiency. Churches are not unlike most businesses I see. They may pride themselves in striving to be more efficient, but they rarely take a hard look at what it is that's keeping them from being more effective, or even analyze what it *means* to be effective. The feedback is often too intimidating."

Gary's tone was somber. "Is it hopeless? Are a certain percentage of businesses and churches destined to be mediocre?"

"I don't think you believe that," Jeff appealed, "and neither do I. The Bible is based upon the idea that people can change by divine intervention, as well as by people working together."

"I agree," said Gary. "It just seems interesting that few churches ever seem to reach their potential, but that's because organizations are sort of just extensions of people. It seems that much of life is focused on paying the bills, getting the kids to school, cleaning the house, and filling our daily planners. But you can get to the end of a year or a lifetime and think, *What did I accomplish? What did I achieve?*"

"Right," Jeff agreed. "We need to determine what we want to be effective at and then pursue it with diligence."

"Okay, I'm all for philosophizing," Gary replied, "but what does this mean on a day-in, day-out basis at Family Church?"

"I think it has everything to do with what we do at our church," responded Jeff. "Before we pour our attention into the details, we need to make sure that we're pursuing the right goals and that we can accomplish those goals. The organizational realm used to be into mission statements, and I've noticed that churches followed the trend. But if you look at most church mission statements, they're much the same. They have to do with elements of worship, fellowship and reaching the world for Christ. But where is the accountability? Are we accomplishing our mission? Mission statements are worthless unless we establish measurable standards."

"Whew, slow down," said Gary. "I'm having brain strain thinking this through. I know you're right. I think the reason so many congregations are reluctant to ask the tough questions is because they fear the answers. But who's going to hold us accountable?"

"Ultimately," Beth stressed, "God is, but don't you think that God gives us the responsibility?"

"I think you're right, Beth," said Gary. "If we don't create a group structure in which the tough questions on effectiveness can be asked, we'll play games and avoid the truth."

"Denial is a strong urge," Jeff added. "The problem is that we're rarely conscious of it when it occurs."

"Okay," Gary's tone was passionate. "Let's get back to the efficiency/effectiveness relationship. How are they the same and how are they different?"

"It's overly simplistic," Jeff explained, "but effectiveness is doing the right thing and efficiency is doing things right. It's usually difficult to be effective when efficiency is low, but high efficiency does not guarantee effectiveness. As we said, you can be making great time going in the wrong direction. Many congregations place a lot of time and energy into ministries and events that yield few long-term results. The problem is that more and more energies go into efficiency and less and less into seeing whether you are still being effective."

"If so many ministries and congregations are lacking effectiveness," asked Beth, "what are they doing wrong?"

"No one can complain about the motives and intentions of most churches," Jeff reasoned. "The bottom line, however, is stewardship. Is this the best use of our time, talent and resources? We have to constantly ask the question as to *why* we are in business. Organizations that don't answer this question ultimately die. For instance, when train companies thought they were in the train business instead of the transportation business, they went broke. When telegraph companies thought they were in the telegraph business, instead of communications, they failed. The church is no different."

"Makes sense," said Gary.

Beth asked, "How do you find that balance where you don't put too much energy into quality at the expense of reducing effectiveness?"

"Like we said before," said Jeff, "it's always a judgment call. That's where measurements come into play. If you can track a ministry, you can get a feel of whether attention to detail is adding or detracting from effectiveness."

Beth was emphatic. "But how do you explain that to your workers? If a church nursery does not take care of little issues like registration, diaper changing and any number of little issues, it will begin to overlook many other details and lose ground with church members."

"That's the accumulative effect," Jeff explained. "Too much dust in an air filter will shut down your air-conditioning system. Too many particles of dirt in a fuel filter will keep the car from running. By helping people see how an attention to detail keeps their ministries running well, we can keep their attention on effectiveness and the big picture."

"Okay," Gary interjected, "so let me play the you-know-who's advocate. When does the pursuit of effectiveness become too large? You often hear about businesses that compromise and use people just to be successful. If effectiveness is our main objective—in ministry or in life—don't you run the risk of selling your soul?"

Jeff paused briefly and rallied his thoughts. "Gary, my argument to that scenario is that effectiveness should not just be a certain measurement, such as profits. We used to think that corporations were either profitable or value driven—that you could not be both. What a growing number of corporations are doing is pursuing values *and* profit.

"We can balance the need for a people-centered business," Jeff elaborated, "and still yield a profit. If you have a staff person who becomes obsolete in one area, you do your best to train and motivate that person to keep him on the team. But if you get to a point where you've exhausted your resources, you have to put the good of the organization above the individual and let that person go. But you do not terminate a person until you've exhausted those resources, if you are a people-oriented organization."

"That makes sense," Gary agreed. "It seems that we've seen so many models of successful ministries or businesses that seem to be productivity oriented at all costs."

"When you're only outcome oriented," said Jeff, "you will tend to compromise on ethical and relational standards. I think that the best, long-term productivity comes by pursuing effective outcomes and processes. It's sort of hypocritical to have quality goals without pursuing quality means."

"Let me see if I'm getting this," said Beth. "The goal of quality improvement is to enhance effectiveness, to accomplish ministry goals. The question that needs to be regularly addressed is: Are we being fruitful? The temptation is to focus on efficiency versus effectiveness. Efficiency should enhance effectiveness, but you have to constantly weigh the amount of resources that goes into being efficient with what it produces."

"Great," said Jeff. "You've got it."

"And you don't need to sell your soul to be productive," said Gary. "You can emphasize quality processes as well as effective outcomes. The issue is more a matter of what it is we want to achieve and what are we willing to do or change to achieve it. Quality is a mind-set, not a certain size or budget. Quality tends to attract people and resources, but is designed to be a means to an end."

"You've got it, too," said Jeff. "A nice facility, glossy brochures, wonderful music and quality child care doesn't necessarily make you effective in ministry. If you're doing things well, but those things do not create effectiveness, then you'd better change what you're doing until you find what *will* make you effective and still in the ministry business."

THE GIST OF IT...
WHY WE DO WHAT WE DO AND THE WAY WE DO IT

In 1 Corinthians 9:19-23, Paul says, "Though I am free and belong to no man, I make myself a slave to everyone, to win as many as possible. To the Jews I became like a Jew, to win the Jews. To those under the law I became like one under the law (though I myself am not under the law), so as to win those under the law. To those not having the law I became like one not having the law (though I am not free from God's law but am under Christ's law), so as to win those not having the law. To the weak I became weak, to win the weak. I have become all things to all men so that by all possible means I might save some. I do all this for the sake of the gospel, that I may share in its blessings."

For Paul, effectiveness in ministry was his bottom line. What's our goal and how can we get there? Efficiency has to do with how we get there—slow, fast, smooth or bumpy. The goal of efficiency is to be effective with the fewest snags and the least resources consumed (time, money, talent) so that we can invest in other areas for even greater effectiveness.

Unfortunately, many congregations resist an honest look at their effectiveness for fear that they will need to change and take risks to become more effective. We assume that change will involve pain, which it often does, and any normal human being avoids voluntarily painful situations.

But Paul recognized that a part of effectiveness usually involved some sort of painful discipline. He continued by saying, "Do you not know that in a race all the runners run, but only one gets the prize? Run in such a way as to get the prize. Everyone who competes in the games goes into strict training. They do it to get a crown that will not last; but we do it to get a crown that will last forever. Therefore I do not run like a man running aimlessly; I do not fight like a man beating the air. No, I beat my body and make it my slave so that after I have preached to others, I myself will not be disqualified for the prize" (1 Cor. 9:24-27).

"Winning the prize" is another phrase for effectiveness. The goal of quality improvement is not necessarily to do what we are doing with more efficiency. The foolish steward in Jesus' parable (see Matt. 25) was very efficient with how he buried his talent. In fact, he saved a lot more energy and took a lot less risk than stewards given two and five talents. But of course, he was called foolish and was tossed out for torment. God holds us accountable for our life and ministry investments. He expects results. He wants us to be effective.

For many of us, if we would just raise the level on a few of our ministry aspects—music, publicity, facilities, message, hospitality, child care, etc.—we would see significant increases in effectiveness. For example, our goal is for our music ministry to provide quality worship music on a consistent basis and to develop the latent talent among our congregation. In other words, we're not just interested in hiring a professional team of backup musicians.

Awhile back, I (Stan Toler) had to talk with our worship pastor whose desire for a top-quality sound was leaving us with hardly anyone to sing or play. I suggested that our intent was to develop people and, if our standards for perfection were too high, then we needed to lower them to invite more people to participate in the music ministry.

At the same time, we knew that not just anyone should be placed in front of a microphone and that we must maintain some semblance of quality. Although we disagreed on the exact level of this adjustment, we talked through the goal of the ministry. Improving the quality of music might lower the quality of talent development. These are the tough decisions that must be made in the week-in, week-out issues of quality ministry improvement.

People who confuse ministry improvement with perfectionism tend to elevate efficiency above effectiveness. The most efficient steward in Jesus' parable was the least effective. Efficiency for efficiency's sake is poor stewardship.

What Paul was talking about in his famous "win some" passage was cultural relevance. As any missionary, he knew that the way to effectiveness was to become like the people he wanted to reach.

People who live in Zimbabwe have different cultural values than people who live in Oklahoma City or Scottsdale. Our goal is to reach people in a certain culture. Even within a single community, you cannot realistically hope to reach everyone. That is why God places different styles of congregations in a cluster effect. But many congregations do not understand the subculture that God has called them to reach.

For example, many believe that they are called to reach the unchurched in their communities, yet a majority of their programs and ministries are structured toward maintaining their present churched attendees. They are not answering the questions that the unchurched are asking. They are not aware of the invisible barriers that keep so many people from walking through the doors once, let alone twice.

Cultural relevance in the twenty-first century means significantly different things than in the 1950s, where so many of our congregations obtained their molds. Cultural relevance is not the same as biblical compromise. These are two separate issues. If you compromise the gospel in hopes of making it more palatable for people, this results in corrupt doctrine and ministry ineffectiveness. What you need to do is translate the good news of Christ into ways that unchurched people can understand. While not compromising on the essence, you have changed the ways in which it is understood by defining the concepts into everyday language that people use.

Jesus did it often via His parables. He told stories from the culture of the people to whom He ministered so that they could envision the kingdom of God. The test for veracity is the bearing of spiritual fruit. If the message you communicate in twenty-first century terms results in changed lives and the fruit of the Spirit (see Gal. 5:22,23), then you have to recognize it as God's blessing.

The people of the twenty-first century are different from previous generations. In America, they are more post-Christian. We cannot assume that they know or trust the Bible, that their underlying theological beliefs are Christian-friendly, or that they even want to understand Christianity the way so many of us did growing up.

Congregations that thrive in the twenty-first century will be those that are perceived as relevant. People in a post-Christian society, who have multiple options vying for their limited attention, will not have the time or patience to pursue activities that fail to make a positive impact in their lives.

Cultural relevance is more than just style; it is also excellence. Taking your tie off, using a praise band instead of a choir, employing drama and tossing lyrics up on a screen is not the same as cultural relevance.

For instance, I (Stan Toler) remember seeing a catchy, four-color glossy brochure for a new church plant in our area. We were not yet leading Sunday morning worship, so we decided to visit this church.

The publicity said we'd experience a classy, contemporary congregation. When we got there, our hopes were flattened. The nursery was poorly staffed. No one greeted us. A few used toys were tossed in a box for the kids to play with. The music was okay, but the room was so huge that it made the few people present feel like BBs in a box. The message was dry, and the pastor, although pleasant, lacked excitement. We left with the impression that we'd been deceived.

The bait-and-switch idea of promising one thing and providing another seemed to fit. If the church had spent half the money on the publicity and invested it in a nicer nursery, training workers, and even finding a location that better fit their size, they would have been better off. The congregation is still struggling to survive, but they have probably not considered quality improvement as a solution to their ineffectiveness.

If God has called your congregation to be a pipe organ, hymn-singing traditional-type church, then do it with excellence. Make it your best. Don't hold back on quality and constant improvement. At the same time, understand that pipe organ radio stations are nonexistent today. Also, very few people wear suits and ties in their weekend activities. King James Elizabethan terminology is found only in Shakespeare classes. But if you firmly believe God has called you to reach traditional Christians, then do not waver from that endeavor.

Perhaps God has given you a desire to reach the unchurched and the baby boomers. It will be necessary to understand and respond to their lifestyles and communication styles. If you don't, you'll be ineffective when there is any cultural diversity in your ministry community. You can only do a few things to reach one or two cultural groups at one time. If you want to be effective with people outside your church, then you will have to take a hard look at the way you go about ministry.

The goal of this chapter is to understand the relationship of effectiveness, efficiency and quality improvement. People sometimes mistake quality concern with efficiency, doing things better. True quality improvement has to do with effectiveness and efficiency, doing the right things better.

A *LEADER MODELS EXCELLENCE.*

M Maintains the mission.
O Oversees the plan.
D Develops more leaders.
E Encourages the heart.
L Loves to celebrate.

QUESTIONS AND ANSWERS

Q. When do we begin to confront the reality that some of our ministries seem to be alive but don't appear to be bearing much fruit?

Alan: Ministry health and fruitfulness can be challenging measurement matters. I once heard a scientist say, "If you can't measure it, it's not." James might agree with that, suggesting that even such hard-to-grasp realities such as faith need to be visible.

You might begin with an in-depth team discussion on what you are trying to accomplish with this ministry. Develop some tangible terms that help you know whether you're doing well or not. You can measure ministry-user response, monitor growth, review periodic surveys, and talk to those who are *not* using the ministry.

Remember, if you say that one of your goals is to reach the lost, do you have a way of monitoring that goal?

There are no shortcuts to any place worth going.
— BEVERLY SILLS

Stan: Many churches are so caught up in traditional programming that they are unable to fulfill the Great Commission. They have many activities and yet few lasting results.

While watching television one evening, I heard Dr. Charles Stanley share a story about a trip he took. He was photographing a beautiful canyon, and while looking for a place to sit down, he slipped and fell. Unfortunately, he broke his left wrist. Amazingly, in his right hand he still held his camera, which had no apparent damage to it.

Dr. Stanley recounted that his traveling companion asked how he held onto the camera. Dr. Stanley replied, "When I went down, I probably instinctively held it up and stuck out my left arm to break my fall."

"The whole situation," said Dr. Stanley, "reminded me of how dependent each member of the physical body is on the other members. My wrist took the shock of the fall. My legs picked me back up. My feet took my injured wrist to safety. My other hand and arm nursed my injury as we made our way out of the canyon." Dr. Stanley concluded, "If the members of our physical bodies acted independently of one another, we would be in a terrible mess!" (*Discipleship Journal*, November/December 1995, pages 38,39.)

The five-star church must function together as one unit in order to achieve team effectiveness. Paul, in Romans 15, reminded believers that he had a responsibility to the believers and the unbelievers. He pleaded for their assistance as partners in ministry to join forces and give the gospel to all people. Quite a model of effectiveness!

Q. What are some ways of comparing efficiency with effectiveness? In other words, when do you know when too much or too little is going into sweating the small stuff?

Stan: Bobb Beihl uses an acrostic, DOCTOR, when consulting with church organizations. Bobb says "play doctor" when you are seeking better results in ministry.

D Diagnosis
O Organization
C Cash
T Tracking
O Overall involvement
R Refinement

What a great formula for measuring ministry effectiveness! In fact, through using this guide, a church could be well on its way to developing a criteria for ministry effectiveness.

Alan: Probably the best way to recognize just the right balance between efficiency and effectiveness is through monitoring the two. You'll hear a lot of church-growth type pastors explain their growth, which may or may not have been the real reasons for the growth. Maybe it was shrewd marketing, maybe exceptional talent, maybe the Holy Spirit, or more than likely, a combination of these and other ingredients. Sometimes, it is more of an interactive chemistry than any single item. Look for trends. Develop a few simple charts. Analyze what it is you're doing differently when you see changes in efficacy.

Q. What if your team members don't agree on how much sweat should go into the small stuff? It seems that some people are prone to be more detail oriented than others.

Alan: Acknowledging concessions and even varying responsibilities based on how strongly a team member feels on a certain task or topic helps create teamwork. Again, monitoring a ministry and measuring effectiveness helps you justify adding or deleting an idea, based on whether it will help or hinder. Training leaders to understand different points of view and personality types can greatly reduce conflict.

Most leader types are not detail oriented, meaning that they need to recruit an assistant who is. People who are too laid back will tend to let sloppiness creep into a ministry. People who are overly perfectionistic will tend to alienate themselves from other team members, and even church members.

Stan: One of my first lessons as a young pastor came in this critical area of communication. While my first tendency was to pull away and try to forget the tense situation, the real answer was to bring the critics together and to try to discuss it in a positive light. This approach has rarely failed me. Generally speaking, people want to get along and reduce tensions that build in church team situations.

Great spirits have always encountered violent opposition from mediocre minds.

— ALBERT EINSTEIN

Q. How do you deal with people who just can't seem to remember why they're in ministry? They get caught up in keeping policies and rules instead of serving people with excellence.

Stan: Some time ago, John Maxwell and I were speaking at a conference in a Southern state. Church leaders had taped homemade signs with event rules on every glass door at each entry point. I was turned off. I like pastor Rick Warren's view on this one. He maintains that we should be *high* on relationships and *low* on rules!

Having been raised in a strict church environment, I felt liberated when I heard Rick make this point. For years I've been saying to the rule makers, "We should be strong in our operations structure and have only a few policies." Therefore, at Trinity Church we only have 13 policies. The way to find balance is through teaching values and beliefs to the ministry team members.

Alan: I remember being chastised one time while on staff at a large church for letting my ministry members drag in nice foyer furniture because we had run out of chairs for a Super Bowl outreach event. The criticism was that we might ruin the expensive furnishings. I asked, "Are we in the people business or the aesthetics business?"

The critic responded, "Both."

"No," I interjected, "we're in the people business, and if we run out of chairs, we should be able to use whatever is nearby." Stories like that can go a long way to communicate values and priorities. Regardless of any organization, the leader's job is to remind people to keep the main thing the main thing. Look for people doing things right and applaud them. Elevate team members who really seem to emulate the type of customer service attitude you want to convey.

Affirm everyone, but don't assume that everyone is on track just because they show up. Jesus spent more time with the Twelve than with the masses, and more time with three apostles than the other nine. Encourage leaders to keep an eye out for team members who represent the main thing of that ministry. Look for potential team members who seem to exhibit the gifts and aptitudes that you want as well.

Then go after them with a personal invitation for ministry. Studies show that 80 percent of people would engage in a ministry task if personally asked. Most people are not self-motivated enough or are inundated with various opportunities to pursue an invitation. The "task of ask" is a responsibility of every effective team leader. Don't rely on announcements. Recruit your potential team members one by one. Jesus employed the one-on-one style of recruitment.

Leaders do the right things.

— WARREN BENNIS

THE DOERS SECTION

- Discuss the differences between efficiency and effectiveness.
- Think of examples of the two concepts in your church.
- Think of a time when effectiveness soared, but efficiency languished.
- Discuss your current standards for effectiveness.
- Discuss potential effectiveness standards for each ministry.
- Brainstorm concerning putting "thorns in our laurels," as it applies to ministry effectiveness.
- Ask: Who will hold us accountable as we strive for ministry effectiveness?

Quality in the Physical Arena

★ ★ ★ ★ ★

*Churches only get one chance to make
a lasting impression!*

—ALAN NELSON

"Let's talk about applying what we've learned about quality improvement in our church," Jeff began. "There are three arenas that we need to think about in terms of quality improvement at Family Church: physical facilities and tools, programs and spiritual growth."

Gary asked, "Is it safe to assume that most quality-improvement principles in business don't include spiritual items?"

"Well," Jeff grinned and replied, "yes and no. Obviously, most organizations do not consider the spiritual quality as we do, but they do concern themselves with corporate culture. A growing number are concerned with the work atmosphere beyond merely the physical. These businesses are seeing people from a more holistic view, and they are open to considering spiritual issues—more than in the past. By far, most are not as biblically based, but spiritual and emotional qualities are part of the mix for these organizations. Since our church is a faith community, we have to measure the quality of our primary service, which is spiritual nurturing."

"That's so wonderful to hear," Gary exclaimed. "The quality-improvement idea has more to do with obvious things such as how facilities look and the professionalism of the music."

"Indeed, quality issues have to do with core values," continued Jeff. "An organization that is about providing top-quality widgets has to measure the quality of them if it is going to pursue excellence. We are no different except that our business is the soul business. We have to be concerned with the caliber of ministries that we provide to help people grow spiritually."

Beth asked, "If so, what do the physical and program arenas have to do with our business?"

"As you'll see," said Jeff, "programs that help us grow spiritually and in the physical arena reflect our self-image and how we minister to people."

"I'm all for that," Gary replied. "I'm tired of Christians feeling that since they are spiritual they don't need to take care of themselves, their place of worship or their ministry environment."

"It's good theology to include the whole person," Jeff reflected, "not just the soul. God talks a lot about our bodies and how we present ourselves."

"Jesus said our bodies are the temples of the Holy Spirit," Beth chipped in.

"True," Jeff agreed, "and our clothes, home and decorations all reflect what we value. More than ever, if we want to reach a secular society, we must elevate our curb appeal."

Gary asked, "What elements of the physical arena should we be concerned about?"

"Let's look at the outside facilities," Jeff noted, "inside facilities, publicity and miscellaneous aspects."

"Fasten your seat belts," Beth smiled. "I've seen most of Majesty Suites' facilities, and I'm afraid we can't touch them in excellence. You have a huge budget to work with, which is usual for a five-star hotel. On the other hand, Family Church is a nonprofit entity. People would become upset if we began spending money on ornate decorations, buildings and landscaping."

"Let's back up a bit," Jeff motioned with his right hand. "I think you may be jumping to conclusions. You're confusing two things—excellence and expense with savings and inexpensiveness. First of all, excellence is a different commodity than expense. Second, you can waste money by saving money when quality is compromised. People are not attracted by mediocre surroundings."

"Okay," Beth nodded, "maybe I did jump to conclusions. Majesty Suites is so impressive, it can be intimidating to those of us in the church world. We assume that we will never be able to compete with the level of excellence in the for-profit realm."

"Beth," Jeff appealed, "I think you've been in business long enough to know that there is just as much mediocrity and lack of excellence in the marketplace as in any faith community. Quality starts as a mind-set and, like our faith, ends up with tangible fruit."

"You're right," Beth conceded. "There is only a small percentage in both realms that stands out. So how can we maximize our assets, Jeff?"

The general manager grinned and pointed to Gary. "Last week, Gary taught us in the parable of the talents that it's not how much we have, but what we do with what we have that counts. This reminds me of the Shakers. They pursue a simple and humble lifestyle, but everyone acknowledges the quality of Shaker furniture. You can be classy without being huge."

"That's a good illustration," said Beth. "I think I know what you mean by savings being different than inexpensiveness, but can you illustrate it, Jeff?"

"Another way of saying it is that many people confuse effectiveness and price. We mentioned this before, but saving a dime here and a buck there is perceived, by some, to be good stewardship. But when the result of saving money is a shoddy brochure or equipment breakdowns, you end up getting less over the long haul. It's kind of like breakfast cereal. If you go just by the size of the box and the price of the cereal, you may be paying more per ounce. A lot of churches waste money because they spend it on poor-quality items instead of investing it in excellence."

Gary nodded affirmingly and asked, "What can we do about improving the quality of our physical arena?"

"Let's start with the first category," Jeff explained, "the external facilities. Our goal is to create a list of everything we see from the outside—signs, paint and landscaping. How we look says a lot about how we feel about ourselves, and how we feel about those who come to our church."

"I'm making a quick list of some things we could do with our outside appearance," said Beth. "What are some specifics I should look for?"

"Well," Jeff replied, "little details begin with landscaping. Are the plants alive, trimmed and fertilized? Is the grass green and mowed? Do we need to hire a landscape architect to enhance our curbside appearance? Does the building need painting? Are the windows clean? Is there adequate signage directing people? Are the signs old-fashioned or up-to-date? Essentially, we want to be a quality neighbor, regardless of what neighborhood we find ourselves in."

"Sometimes it's easy to overlook things that you've gotten used to," said Gary. "I suppose that a secret shopper or someone new could give us ideas on beautifying our facility."

"Absolutely," agreed Jeff. "We have corporate people who come in two, three times a year to give Majesty Suites a demanding white glove test. We can develop similar teams to do that for our church."

"Great," Beth responded, "but what about inside facilities, Jeff?"

"Our inside list should include things such as signs pointing visitors to the nursery and Sunday School, even the worship center. Is the decor of our auditorium, foyer and classrooms dated? We can't expect people who shop in some of the nicest malls and department stores to suddenly drop their standards. For help in this area, maybe we need to find someone in the church who demonstrates good taste in their own home or business to give us some ideas."

"I think our goal is to create environments that evoke natural responses from people," said Beth. "We want our guests to say, 'Wow, I feel good about this place.' We do that through getting the right lighting, color schemes, comfortable seating and decor enhancements."

"This all sounds great," Gary said, "but I keep thinking, What's this going to cost us?"

Jeff was emphatic. "The stewardship question is not, What is this going to cost us, but, What is this going to cost us if we don't improve?"

Gary conceded, "Most churches tend to ask the wrong questions when considering improvements and costs."

"I think so," Jeff commented. "My suggestion would be to start constructing a list of interior items that might need a review and also use a secret shopper or person from outside our church to give us their impressions on things we might have overlooked."

"Good," replied Gary as he began a new line of thought. "Impressions are important, Jeff. So, let me ask you, how are our publications connected with quality in the physical arena?"

"The matter of publicity is more a concern for creating a visual image for the church," said Jeff. "Our publications say a lot about who we are as a congregation."

Beth asked, "What do you mean by publicity? Do you mean like an information packet?"

Jeff explained, "I mean everything we print—information brochures, our Sunday worship folders and our monthly newsletter."

Beth questioned, "Aren't worship folders and newsletters more in-house items than publicity outreach?"

"You don't know where every piece you print, copy or mail lands," Jeff replied. "Besides, it's all publicity! People carry around worship folders, put newsletters on their refrigerators and hand out printed materials to friends outside our church. We want our people to feel proud of where they worship as well as communicate excellence in all that we do."

"I've noticed that Majesty Suites has a wonderful brochure and information packet," Beth commented.

"I'll have you know that we have invested a lot of time and money to create a five-star image on paper," said Jeff. "Naturally, you don't want to promise more than you can provide, which is the old false-advertising issue. Never underestimate the importance of a well-constructed worship folder, newsletter, brochure, letterhead, business card or mailer."

Gary pleaded, "How can we compete with all the four-color, glossy pieces that businesses commonly use for their work? It seems like everyone is raising the bar so high that churches can't compete."

"Because everyone is doing it, the church cannot do anything less," Jeff reflected. "The expectations of society have been raised, right or wrong. We have to reach people who judge us by what they see, which is often through publicity and written literature. I've seen so many shoddy newsletters, cheap-looking bulletins and hokey-looking church ads that it wouldn't take much to shine in this area. Why do we have anything less to offer the community than Majesty Suites or Xerox or Target? They understand the importance of contemporary graphics, color printing and sharp literature to make a good presentation. Churches have the life-changing gospel of Christ to offer people. We've got to understand the importance of presenting ourselves well on the printed page."

"I agree with you, Jeff," said Beth. "I've seen more ugly church newsletters than I can imagine. But are you saying that if we can't do it well, we shouldn't do it at all?"

"Yes, I am," said Jeff. "Every mediocre piece of publicity reflects who we are and communicates a lack of quality. Quality improvement must become a part of every aspect of our ministry, which includes how we present ourselves through printed communication. Audiotape and videotape productions fall in this category as well."

Gary asked, "Should we have outside people analyze us in this area, too?"

"Yes," Jeff replied, "but I think that we would do well to gather graphic artists and printers in our congregation who can give us ideas on improving the quality of our publicity."

"Outside facilities, inside facilities and publicity," Gary noted. "What other areas in the physical arena do we need to review, Jeff?"

"If it is touchable or can be seen, we need to check it for quality. Obviously, paint, carpet, furniture, classroom equipment, water fountains and rest rooms are parts of the physical arena. Even the food presented at fund-raiser banquets or women's teas is important."

Beth smiled. "I've certainly noticed that Capers restaurant does a beautiful job of presenting its buffet."

"That's because we understand that people don't just come to eat," said Jeff. "People also come to have a culinary experience, and part of that experience comes from the food's presentation. Does the food look appetizing? Does it look fresh?"

Gary asked, "What else?"

"The physical can be applied to the way the staff presents itself," replied Jeff. "How do our hospitality greeters dress and look? Is our nursery staff dressed in professional-looking smocks, or are they dressed in T-shirts with disheveled hair? Looking to the business community, dress codes vary. Disney does not allow facial hair. IBM is known for its suit-and-tie image. McDonald's employees wear uniforms. We need to think through how we are appearing to the people we serve, which can mean we are concerned with our appearance."

"That does it," said Gary. "I'm not shaving off my mustache."

The three laughed.

"Think about it," said Jeff. "The goal is not to dress up, but rather to dress like the people to whom you are ministering. That is a basic of being mission-minded. But whether it's blue-jean casual or suit and tie, looking nice and appearing professional is a matter of quality. When chefs wear white smocks and tall white hats, that makes a difference in how they feel about themselves and how people perceive them, even though only a few customers ever see chefs work in the kitchen."

"Okay," Beth responded, "I guess it's time to increase our clothing expense account. How about it, Gary?"

"I'm sorry," Gary shook his head and continued, "maybe it's my Dutch frugality, but my mind moves back to the dollar signs."

"Most people think about cost," Jeff nodded, "which is fine. We have to be realistic. Let me give you one idea that might help. Instead of purchasing five $175 suits, invest in two $400 suits and wear them more often. Quality clothing lasts longer and looks nicer. For a new church worshiping in a school or other rented facility, they could put extra money into a professional exhibit display and top-quality brochures and information folders. By communicating touches of quality, the people attending the service will know that excellence is recognized, even though current finances may not allow for much more."

"I think we could do with some touches around Family Church," said Gary.

"Sure, every church can," Jeff exclaimed. "At Majesty Suites, we have a marble check-in counter and giant courtyard fountain. Your eye goes toward the 'touch of class' we provide for our guests. For a church, it might be a work of art or a statue in our foyer. Obviously, we should invest more money in what people see and use often than behind-the-scene items and locations which are rarely seen or used. Our storerooms don't have to have nice carpet and granite countertops, but our foyer and meeting rooms do."

"A touch here, a touch there," said Gary. "We could do that."

Then King David said to the whole assembly: "My son Solomon, the one whom God has chosen, is young and inexperienced. The task is great, because this palatial structure is not for man but for the Lord God. With all my resources I have provided for the temple of my God—gold for the gold work, silver for the silver, bronze for the bronze, iron for the iron and wood for the wood, as well as onyx for the settings, turquoise, stones of various colors, and all kinds of fine stone and marble—all of these in large quantities. Besides, in my devotion to the temple of my God I now give my personal treasures of gold and silver for the temple of my God, over and above everything I have provided for this holy temple" (1 Chron. 29:1-3).

THE GIST OF IT...
WHY WE DO WHAT WE DO AND THE WAY WE DO IT

Anthropologists tell us that our physical surroundings—housing, buildings, decorations and attire—reflect how we think about ourselves. Our self-image is directly related to how we value and think of others. Jesus said, "Love your neighbor as yourself" (Matt. 19:19). Providing for people physically is an important part of ministry. The "cup of water" is a tangible expression of grace. While our society has often overemphasized the importance of looks and appearances, we cannot reject this influence by suggesting that there is no need to pursue quality in the physical arena.

Every ministry must come to terms with a balance between aesthetics and pragmatics. The general rule is that churches tend to shoot below the level at which they are called to minister. Even lower-economic congregations can invest sweat equity to spruce up a churchyard, building and sanctuary. The idea that cleanliness is next to godliness gives us an idea of how we need to manage our physical arena.

The economics of quality is that excellence usually attracts finances. Obviously, quality facilities alone will not build a church. We all know about spectacular buildings that stand empty and shoddy buildings that overflow with people. Yet Solomon's Temple, blessed by God, was the best of their day. "Whatever you do, work at it with all your heart, as working for the Lord, not for men" (Col. 3:23).

I (Alan Nelson) love the story about the three bricklayers who were asked what they were making. The first responded, "I'm making

$15 dollars an hour." The second answered, "I'm making a building." The third said, "I'm making a beautiful cathedral, which will reflect the glory of God and provide a place of worship for His people." The third was fired because he was supposed to be building a garage, but you get the point. God deserves our best.

Stewardship means that I constantly weigh the productivity for investment. Different congregations reaching specific people groups will need to vary the level of physical quality. The socioeconomic level of Scottsdale, Arizona, requires us to invest in a higher level of quality simply because the people we are striving to minister to are accustomed to finer things—and can afford them. At the same time, our use of a simple elementary school cafeteria and an adjacent Boys' and Girls' Club gymnasium as church facilities make it impossible for us to replicate the niceties of homes and businesses. People in our congregation accept the differences, however, because our church is new and because we work hard at providing quality in other areas. Down the road, as our church expands and matures, we'll need to invest in bigger-ticket items like facilities and landscaping.

Let's face the facts. We must seek to glorify God in every aspect of ministry!

—ALAN NELSON

QUESTIONS AND ANSWERS

Q. How do we communicate the idea that quality improvement is a mind-set when it's so easy to see dollar signs?

Alan: I think the first thing for people to see is that there is a need for quality improvement in the physical arena. Most congregations don't get to the money issue because they don't see the chipped paint, shoddy landscaping and crooked newsletter layout in the first place. Once the needs have arisen, then you can estimate costs and brainstorm on ways of improving without significant finances. Plus, fund-raising often follows pet projects. For example, if the nursery needs to be renovated or a parent-paging system purchased, sharing the need with parents or grandparents of nursery children will often free up funds that would not come in regular offerings.

Stan: When I became pastor of Oklahoma City First Church of the Nazarene in the early 1980s, the church was struggling financially, although they had just built a beautiful sanctuary! Besides, the educational wing was the "pits." It had shag carpets, walls that needed paint, etc.

I decided to invite the whole church to a Sunday evening meeting. About 60 people showed up. I carefully communicated the need for quality facilities and challenged the group to brainstorm with me. Through that experience I discovered that Dave Sutherland of INJOY Stewardship Services was right: "People give to what captures their imagination."

As our property improvement meeting unfolded, one man stood up and said, "I'll buy the paint for every classroom if teachers will oversee the painting of the rooms." Another man donated $3,000 for flowers and lawn care, and many volunteered services from their businesses.

Q. Where do we start? There are so many things that need to be done, and we might not all agree on where to begin.

Stan: Take a walk through the entire church facility, then go outdoors and look over the grounds. Form a ministry action team and begin discussing the most pressing needs. Prioritize the needs on a scale of 1 to 10 and agree to get started on the top 5 areas.

Alan: Every war zone hospital has a triage area where cases are diagnosed for their severity in comparison with the others. Go for the important projects first, the ones that will benefit the most. Putting up new wallpaper in the staff rest room is not likely to get as much attention as refurbishing the public women's rest room. Better yet, start with the outside because if the community perceives the church as a mediocre ministry, they're not apt to visit the church.

Q. Who should decide what type of changes should be made and where do you allow for individual differences, like color schemes?

Alan: Obviously, you'll need to begin with the decision makers in the church who will ultimately say yes or no to quality-improvement issues. Your consultants ought to be those who have demonstrated expertise in this area. Printers and graphic artists in the church can provide ideas for publicity and literature. Find the parishioners who have neat, well-decorated homes and offices, and invite them to serve on the facility decor team. Seek out sharp dressers to give ideas on volunteer and paid staff attire. Items such as color and decor tend to be emotional items, so be prepared for some differences in opinion.

Stan: I would start with the outside of the church buildings and paint everything that needs it. Then I would move to the church lawn and improve the landscaping, adding colorful flowers. Plus, I would improve church signage. I love signs that make people feel welcome. With apologies to David Letterman, I have my own Top Ten Amusing Church Signs List:

10. The Lite Church...everything you wanted in a church and less!
9. Stop in for a Faith Lift!
8. If you are tired of sin...come on in!
7. Our Sundays are better than Dairy Queen's!
6. Bean Supper tonight...music to follow.
5. Home of the discount tithe.
4. Sign broke...come inside for message.
3. Where will you be sitting in eternity...smoking or nonsmoking?
2. There's no church like this church...this must be the church.
1. Don't let worry kill you...let our church help!

Q. How do you justify spending money on "a touch" when other areas of ministry are lagging?

Stan: I would illustrate by using a local restaurant that has changed hands recently. I would tell the church leaders about the facility improvements that they have made and how it has impacted their ability to attract customers. Be sure to employ the following three tips when planning your strategy:

- Know your own style and uniqueness.
- Utilize your current resources.
- Share your vision with the ministry team.

Alan: Money to provide a touch of class here and there can often be raised outside the general offerings and budgets by sharing the idea and vision with quality-minded people who have financial resources beyond most. Even pursuing outside help from a graphic artist or vendor in exchange for recognition or a tax deduction will work.

Anyone who has traveled through Europe knows the incredible cathedrals situated in some modest surroundings. I used to think critically about such use of money amid so many social needs. But I'm reminded about the time the woman spent so much money on anointing Jesus' feet. By pooling their money, the peasants of hundreds of years ago created a beautiful, grand edifice to bring glory to God.

Always give people the resources to get the job done!
— S T A N   T O L E R

THE DOERS SECTION

- Discuss why it is helpful to understand quality improvement in the physical, program and spiritual arenas.
- Does a holistic approach relieve us from the fear of perceiving quality and excellence only in terms of the tangible?

- Who will make a list of the external items for quality improvement?
- How will the items on the list be analyzed to measure quality?
- Who will check the list (secret shopper or outsider) to see if the outside view agrees or disagrees with our insider's report?
- When will this list be completed and who will review it?
- How will we prioritize work and suggest to improve the quality?
- Are there any "touches" of class needed immediately?

O Lord our God, as for all this abundance that we have provided for building you a temple for your Holy Name, it comes from your hand, and all of it belongs to you (1 Chron. 29:16).

Quality in the Program Arena

★ ★ ★ ★ ★

As your strategy moves toward the future, your
organizational capabilities must move with it.

— D A V E   U L R I C H

Jeff clapped his hands, grinned at his friends, and asked, "All right, are we ready to scale the walls around the next arena for quality improvement?"

Beth chuckled, "I brought my pitons and grappling hook today."

Gary was enthusiastic. "Let's do it."

"We may get a little," Jeff hesitated, "how should I say it?—personal. The arena of programs is an emotional hotbed for those running the ministry or performing the event."

Gary asked, "Jeff, what are we talking about when we say the 'program arena'?"

"Remember, the physical arena has to do with observable items. The program arena has more to do with how we use these tools to minister to people."

"Okay," Gary replied, "I think I see the difference. But how important are events? Are they really effective?"

"That has a lot to do with what we said in previous meetings about efficiency and effectiveness," Jeff responded. "Granted, a church ministry can appear to be operating smoothly, but it may not be meeting needs. Our goal is to analyze what we're doing, as well as the process of how we're doing it. That's very important, especially in a faith community."

Beth asked, "Can you give me a starter list of programs?"

"Sure," Jeff replied. "You can begin with nearly every individual ministry and then break them into a list of events, programs or ministry events. In children's ministry, for example, you can look at the various age-group classes, Sunday morning programs and mid-week events. I would try to break down a program analysis into four main points: staffing, resources, goals and process."

Jeff continued, "Staffing involves asking questions such as: What is the talent and motivation of the people involved in carrying out the ministry? Are they well trained? On the other hand, resources takes a look at equipment and facilities that are the tools for the ministry. Even a good mechanic performs poorly if he does not have adequate tools."

Gary interjected, "What about goals and process?"

"Goals," Jeff explained, "allow us to know when we've hit or missed the target. Having a goal forces us to see whether we have made progress in a specific ministry. Process, however, examines whether people are working as a team and if the leader is proving to be competent, loving and strong."

"That sounds pretty involved, Jeff," responded Gary. "Do you do this on an ongoing basis at Majesty Suites?"

"We do," responded Jeff, "but for us at the hotel, it has become second nature. For us as a church, we need to break down the various components. When programs fail to reach a desirable level of excellence, you can usually narrow it down to something within the aforementioned categories."

"Okay," Gary acknowledged, "let's take a look at the biggie—the Sunday morning worship service. I'll be a sacrificial lamb."

Beth teased, "Martyr complex, huh?"

"Not really, Beth," said Gary. "But Jeff, how would you go about looking at it from a program analysis?"

"Well, let's look at the four categories. First of all, do we have the most talented people running the sound board, singing the solos, playing in the band, and leading the worship?"

Gary added, "And delivering the message?" Laughter rippled through the conference room.

"Yes," Jeff smiled, "I think you are a wonderful communicator, but a growing number of churches are expanding their teaching teams to include staff members and gifted laypeople who can effectively support the senior pastor. A strong leader recognizes team members who have the ability to teach."

Gary commented, "I've been to more than a few churches where they should have added teaching staff."

"It takes a secure leader to share the stage," said Jeff.

Beth questioned, "How do you let a soloist or pianist know that maybe, just maybe, they are not the person for the task?"

"First, you begin by creating a culture of quality awareness and improvement," said Jeff. "You remind people from time to time that our goal is to connect with God. When people are not able to provide the caliber of ministry that is needed, then the church will do its best to train, stretch and find a place where their gifts are best utilized. The opportunities we provide should be based on the abilities people have, not how much money they give or how long they've been in the church."

"Whew, look who's preaching," said Gary.

"I try to practice what I preach," Jeff reacted passionately. "I'm frequently advancing staff members who perform well and deserve to be given more opportunities. I'm also constantly trying to find areas where people of lesser ability can shine well. The goal is the good of the congregation above that of the individual. Our individualistic culture here in America precludes us from accepting this, but when we compromise, we lower the ministry value to many individuals."

Gary replied, "But what if you don't have anyone better to replace someone?"

"That's a judgment call," said Jeff. "If you need the ministry or service, you do the best you can. If you don't need it, you look at your options."

"Does that mean if you don't have an adequate soloist," Beth inquired, "you don't have a solo?"

"Generally speaking, yes," said Jeff. "Quality would suggest that if you cannot do it with a semblance of excellence, you ought not do it, Beth."

She responded, "What role do motivation and talent play?"

"Jesus seemed to pick people who were highly motivated and who had aptitude," Jeff replied, "more often than He did those who were already polished. Quality must include character, attitude and motivation."

"Staffing," Beth continued, "is not the only area to analyze when it comes to evaluating quality in a program. You mentioned resources, too."

"True, another thing to ask ourselves: Is the ministry well resourced? Do we have the right tools? You can't make people sound good with a mediocre sound system. Dingy lighting and shoddy decor in the sanctuary do lower program quality."

Beth asked, "So what do we do?"

"Earlier," Jeff elaborated, "when we were discussing effectiveness, we talked about ministry goals. A lot of people never establish a bull's-eye because they don't want to be held accountable if they miss it. Sadly, too many churches just do church the way they've always done it. To be effective you must set goals."

"I think you did a great job explaining the concept of effectiveness," said Gary. "You also mentioned how the process in creating quality is a critical component."

"You're right," said Jeff. "You have a good memory. The category of process analysis looks at how we prepare and do activities, events and projects. Do we have adequate time for sound checks and rehearsals? Much communication and detail work must go into a well-run service that most people never consider. After every service, we must adequately review and ask what went right, what went wrong, and discuss what we can do to improve it the next time around."

"A lot of this has to fall on leadership," Gary commented. "Do we have the right person as team leader?"

"That's a crucial question," Beth agreed.

"You're right," said Jeff. "Leadership is the most important ingredient for an effective quality team, especially when you're trying to implement significant changes."

"Most of the scenarios that we've been describing have to do with reviewing existing programs and events," said Gary. "But what if we're missing an important ministry area? How do you critique a nonexistent program?"

Jeff explained, "A quality-improvement mind-set will frequently ask the questions, What are we doing now that we need to stop doing? and What are we *not* doing that needs to be done? In other words, do our programs adequately represent our niche within the community? Remember: God is not redundant. Various types of churches aren't placed into the same community to reach identical groups of people with identical programs. In the same way here at Majesty Suites, we are not intimidated by the two-star, three-star and four-star hotels in our area because we provide a unique service for our area."

"Yes, but that's easy to say when you're the only five-star hotel in the area," said Gary. "You're the one that people try to emulate. You hold a unique position that others long for."

"Good point," Jeff acknowledged, "but even if there was another four- or five-star hotel in our area, it would make us even sharper, requiring us to provide even more exceptional value for our customers. The point is, we are a five-star hotel because we are always striving to get better and change according to the needs of the marketplace."

Beth questioned, "What if you find that a certain service or program is not working for you?"

"We change or drop it," said Jeff emphatically.

"That sounds easy for a corporation, but dropping a ministry or church program is not so easy," said Beth. "A faith community is more of a family culture with all the emotions, relationships and feelings."

"True," Jeff conceded, "but when we develop a quality-improvement culture in our church, we will find that people will be much more willing to make changes when necessary to improve a ministry. From what I've read—and from the conferences I've attended with you—that's pretty much how thriving congregations achieve quality."

"I think we must become bolder in the church," Gary sighed. "We must lovingly challenge our set of assumptions about what it means to be a church and to be effective in ministry."

Jeff nodded. "If we take a quality look at all your existing programs and compare them to the vision and calling of our specific church, we will naturally become more effective. We don't need to replicate what a neighboring congregation is doing, if they are doing it well and are filling a niche. There are too many needs for us to compete with other churches. Five-star churches look for unique needs to fill and pursue them with confidence and excellence."

Find a need and fill it!
— ROBERT SCHULLER

THE GIST OF IT...
WHY WE DO WHAT WE DO AND THE WAY WE DO IT

Quality improvement in the program arena is more challenging and rewarding than the physical arena because this is what ministry is about—people. Developing your people assets is the most strategic move for church leaders. Ministry is nothing less than dispensing God's grace. The better we get at it, the more efficient and effective we become at being vessels and tools through whom God's Spirit works.

Ministry doesn't just happen. Concern for quality, as we have been saying all along, begins by creating a quality-oriented environment that has a good chance at dealing with some of the issues that crop up. Anyone in church work knows that sensitivity comes into play when you begin to critique and make changes in various ministries and events. While corporate America commonly downsizes, innovates and adjusts, churches are less adaptive, mainly because we're dealing with volunteers who are in relationships with each other beyond a purely professional level.

The first category to consider is staffing. Do you have the best people in the right positions? There are no wrong people; just wrong positions. The leader's job is to help people find the place of ministry that will best utilize their gifts, skills and passions. The "warm body" approach to filling ministry roles is counterproductive and nonbiblical. Scriptures clearly teach the concept of varying gifts and roles for the purpose of building up the Body.

When we compromise the quality of a ministry for the sake of an individual member, we lower it. Allowing Jane to sing a solo because she's done it for years even though she's not a very strong singer subjects a large group of people to mediocrity. You can help Jane find a place to use her gifts where they will be enhanced, such as an ensemble or choir that matches her ability level.

Ministry agreements become helpful tools in recruiting and holding ministry members accountable (see appendix D). A ministry agreement allows a person to know exactly what the ministry role entails, including to whom the person answers, fundamental skills required, time commitments, and how much training will be provided by the church. A ministry agreement attracts people who know there is a start and a stop point. Such an agreement also makes it easier for us to exit people who may not demonstrate the ability needed for a quality ministry.

Most churches are notorious for recruiting a Sunday School

teacher, tossing her a teacher's guide, and wishing her God's best. How do we know if she is good at what she does—even if she is a public schoolteacher? The public school might prioritize control and content, while the church prioritizes care and process, but you won't know until you interview and monitor her in action.

Who do you have providing the initial training and orientation? Your first choice is to have your best ministry member do the training. Is there a formal assignment of a mentor for the first few weeks, when the new ministry member will have questions and perhaps require some individual attention? Is this apprenticeship period communicated at the start, so there is accountability and understanding?

A quality-improvement culture recognizes these processes as normal. Trying to do this outside of this culture runs the risk of offending volunteers who feel—because they are volunteering or have experience in a similar setting—that they are above apprenticeship and orientation.

In addition to initial training, do we provide for continuing education? If doctors, psychologists, nurses, teachers and salespeople are required to attend continuing education classes, do we do the same for our ministry members? Some churches will send a few paid professionals to conferences and seminars, but most underestimate the importance of sending unpaid ministry teams.

Do we take our teachers to Sunday School conventions, bring in local experts on teaching, or provide a child psychologist to answer questions regarding class behavior and discipline? Do we send our audiovisual members to AV conventions or even arrange a cross-town trip to talk to another church staff with a more advanced system? Do we pass along articles, suggest books, and mail copies of cassettes that can help those in ministry?

A third item related to people is how good we are at finding places in which people can excel. Our job is twofold: creating quality ministries by developing quality staff members and developing people in their own gifts. Churches typically have a limited number of ministry roles. Once a ministry is filled, they put people on a waiting list or just fail to enroll new folks.

This concept is debilitating because it does not go far enough in developing people. Since the goal of the Church is not just to provide ministry events and services but also to develop people, we must constantly seek ways to do this. Most churches only provide ministry roles for approximately 20 to 40 percent of the people who actively attend. This leaves 60 to 80 percent of people inactive and underdeveloped.

We assume that if we fill our 20 to 40 percent need, then we've accomplished our goal, but if our goal is to develop all of our people, we have missed the mark. The responsibility of leadership is to constantly open up new areas of ministry in which people can utilize their gifts and interests. Matching church needs with people is one thing, but creating fresh entrepreneurial ventures to attract and develop more people is another. Most churches are internally oriented, focusing their attention on their own existence. By harnessing the majority left underdeveloped, we provide incredible outreach opportunities that enhance our total ministry as well.

Another category for program/event analysis is resources. For instance, read the following conversation:

"Doctor, here's an ax and a butter knife. You can go ahead and perform this appendectomy. The patient has a need, and we're glad you're here. Now take the ax and butter knife and get started."

This is an exaggeration, but that's how some churches do business—the resources are just not there. Are there dry markers and erasers at the white board? Are their enough VCRs, overheads, copy machines, chairs and tables? Although many of these items may not be in the budget, compiling an inventory of haves and have nots is the beginning point of quality improvement. Prioritizing needs, allowing people to know of these specific needs, and shopping sales are all good stewardship steps for quality improvement.

One of the most overlooked equipping items is the ministry budget. A good rule of thumb is that you shouldn't bring on a part-time or full-time paid staff person until you can cover that individual's salary and sustain an adequate ministry budget. One of the greatest frustrations is for talented people to have their hands tied because they do not have the resources to unleash their creativity.

If we nickel-and-dime our creative types, we risk losing them and their ideas. The same goes for volunteer ministry leaders. We do well to grant adequate ministry budgets so our ministry directors don't have to compromise on quality. Obviously, accountability and cash flow systems need to be implemented. The dual benefit is actual ministry resource enhancement, plus the empowerment of a resourced staff.

An additional category for ministry improvement is to objectively look at our ministry objectives. In a "Peanuts" cartoon, Charlie Brown shoots arrows into a fence, then draws circles around them.

Linus says, "Charlie Brown, that's not how you target shoot."

"I know," responds Charlie. "But this way I never miss." Too many of us go about ministry this way.

We do what we've always done without thinking about what we are striving to accomplish. A transformational process for many churches on the road to excellence would be to answer this question: Why are we in business? If we don't know where we're going, how will we know how to get there or when we've arrived?

Do our present ministries reflect the core values and ministry niche of a church as a whole? If not, they should be removed or at least reduced in emphasis. What new ministries need to be developed or existing ministries empowered? Aligning what we say is important with where we spend money. This has a lot to do with ministry integrity. Measuring our ministry effectiveness is also crucial. When we create budgets and plan our calendar, every item should come under the same considerations: Does it reflect our core values and our ministry vision? Are we doing the process well? Do we work as a team? Is there a competent, loving, strong leader in place? When we accomplish the goal, are people alienated and stressed out?

Addressing the issues of effectiveness and efficiency has much to do with program improvement. We spend time doing things that do not matter or make little difference. We need to be careful not to confuse ministry operations with task accomplishment since our goal is to accomplish something via the ministry. Our programs, services and ministry events are basically conduits to accomplish certain goals. If these goals are not being accomplished, then we're merely playing church, pretending to be something we're not. These may sound like harsh words, but stewardship of time, talent and money are demanding issues in God's kingdom.

Living in obedience to His specific call for our church is our responsibility. God calls no one to mediocrity. When we're dealing with the eternal destiny of people and matters of the heart, we must not do "business as usual." Nothing is more important than the fulfillment of the Great Commission. Sacrificing familiar ministries that are unproductive and making changes in personnel, equipment and style are at the core of Christianity.

QUESTIONS AND ANSWERS

Q. You don't understand my ministry context. My people seem in love with their ministries just the way they are. How am I going to convince them that we need to raise the bar?

Alan: We go back to the same basics, don't we? These are issues of vision, leading and values. We are not suggesting anything other than what Jesus did in His parable of the talents. We are also recognizing that you can't change people who don't want to be changed; Jesus couldn't.

The concept of free will has to be considered. Pastors and church leaders must consider the stewardship of their time and energies in situations that are not likely to change. But the average pastoral tenure of two to four years does not allow for the type of transformational changes we're suggesting in quality improvement.

One of the best ways to induce change is to create an environment of quality. This environment is hard to argue against. Various ministries will begin generating proposed changes when the environment establishes ministry targets, measures effectiveness, and discusses the difference between goals and reality. Moreover, these ministries will begin to build a history of successes—a track record of winning events and projects. The more changes and wins that come about, the more people are motivated to raise the bar themselves.

Stan: I like to draw the parallel between the business community and the Church. The business community markets with a focus on *location.* We need to focus on *relationships.* Big business markets the *cost* of items. We need to call for *commitment.* The business community relies on heavy *advertising.* We need some *satisfied* saints who will go out and tell the community about Christ.

Q. What if you just don't have the talent or the resources to make improvements where they are needed?

Stan: Tough situation, but not impossible! In fact, I faced this as a church planter and then at another church. I had a church that was high on commitment, yet lacking in musical talent. I began by bringing in various guest artists to the church. Many musicians lived in the area, so I leaned on them to sing for our church with a promise of better compensation in the future.

They agreed, and there came a day when we paid them well. Alan is so right in saying "quality begets quality." Because of the influence of the artists, we soon had talent springing up everywhere.

Alan: Start where you are. As the song says, come "Just As I Am." Confess sins of mediocrity and poor stewardship but go and sin no more. The process of quality improvement is not intended to beat us up and make us feel guilty. Nor is it intended to frustrate us with the lack of talent and resources we currently see. The biblical lesson here is that like begets like. To begin the process of quality improvement, do what you can to improve what you can, where you can, when you can. Initial attempts at improvement can be minute, but the goal is not so much to improve as it is to prime the pump for improving.

You want to start small and model the process and benefit of improving a ministry or service. Maybe it's painting a tired exterior, or planting some flowers or shrubs. It could be a new piece of furniture in the foyer or nursery that you strategically had donated. You may raise the lights, open the windows, or make the worship service transitions smoother. There are likely a multitude of ways that a church can begin to make improvements that will tend to create an atmosphere of improvement. Excellent people are attracted to quality. Excellence brings out the best in all of us, motivating us to do our best.

Q. Okay, we've come to the conclusion that our staff member or pastor just does not have what it takes to get us to where we need to go. How do we go forward?

Alan: The first question I'd ask is, How do we know this person is the one holding us back from raising the quality bar? Sometimes leaders and staffers become scapegoats for underlying system problems. We assume that a new person in the role will make a difference while we live in denial of our own deeper issues within a church.

The second question I'd ask is, Have we done all we can do to motivate and stretch this staff person? One job of the organization is to do what it can to help the staffer (paid or volunteer) to reach his or her potential. Sometimes organizations give up too early or assume that they are merely recipients versus investors in good staff.

The final questions I'd ask before hiring or recruiting a replacement are: Why did this person not take us where we wanted to go? Did we recruit well the first time? Did the organization outgrow the person? Do we have blind spots that are keeping us from finding the right person for the right spot? Having overturned these stones, I'd launch forward because the fruitfulness of a group cannot be compromised for an individual.

Stan: You're painfully right. Bite the bullet and deal with the "squatters on the east side of Jordan." It will only hold the church back if you let a nongrowth person continue to flounder. On the other hand, we must give our best effort in trying to bring everyone with us on the success journey to the five-star church. I would highly recommend using the following formula for quality encouragement that I learned years ago:

Coaching...helping the church team succeed.
Consulting...providing great wisdom and counsel.
Cheerleading...creating a great atmosphere.
Coordinating...the flow and process.

Q. Who should be on a program analysis team?

Stan: Balance is the key. You need a leader, someone who is analytical, and a creative person to be on the program analysis team. I highly recommend keeping the group small.

Alan: I think the bigger question is how much change needs to take place. Naturally, the ministry leader, key participants and a few regular church members should meet from time to time to discuss issues of effectiveness, quality and improvement. If we don't include all three types of participants (leaders, key players, church members), we run the risk of blind spots. From time to time, an outside consultant can greatly benefit a church.

THE DOERS SECTION

- Develop a list of the organized ministries and the varying events, services and programs each is responsible for during the church calendar year.
- Designate a responsible person for each ministry, event and service provided.
- Discuss the purpose of your church. Can you measure effectiveness based on your purpose?

- Ask:
    1. What is the purpose of a specific ministry and event?
    2. Which ministries or events are doing well?
    3. Which ministries or events need quality improvement?
    4. How is the quality of our staffing? How do we recruit, train and assess ministry members?

- List resource items needed to enhance the quality of each ministry or event.

    Consider the following:
    A. Top priority
    B. Highly recommended
    C. Wish list

- Why are these items on each list and how do we justify placing them there? In other words, on what am I basing my estimate of quality improvement?
- What new programs and ministries do we need to consider to make us more effective as a church as a whole?
- Which existing programs/ministries do we need to let go of?
- What have we learned about finding and developing ministry leaders?

C h a p t e r
12

Quality in the Spiritual Arena

✪ ✪ ✪ ✪ ✪

*They devoted themselves to the apostles' teaching
and to the fellowship, to the breaking of bread
and to prayer.*

ACTS 2:42

Jeff looked across the table at Beth and Gary. His mind was churning over what he was about to share in this next training session. "I'd like to invest a whole meeting on how to measure spiritual growth," he said.

Beth questioned, "Isn't measuring spiritual growth tough to do?"

"I'm sure it's difficult," Gary added. I think that's why pastors get hung up on numbers and why others burn out—it is difficult to measure soul growth. When you build a house or write a sermon, you can see the progress and measure your success. However, growing people and measuring ministerial success is a slow process."

"True," Jeff said, "but how did Jesus measure spiritual growth?"

Gary was puzzled. "What do you mean?"

Beth interjected, "One thing Jesus valued was reaching the lost."

"Good point," Jeff replied. "Let's start with that. One way we can measure spiritual growth, since that is a core value for us, is to see how many people come to Family Church who did not know

Christ prior to attending. This is somewhat measurable, in terms of tracking decisions to follow Christ or compiling a list of individuals who did not come from strong churches."

Beth added, "Another way the Bible measures growth is via service—getting involved in ministry."

"Great point, Beth," said Jeff. "If getting involved in ministry is a core value—you grow your soul by serving others—we can measure how many people get involved in an ongoing ministry; we can measure how many people discover their gifts in the process. By surveying ministry effectiveness and counting the number of people involved in a ministry, we can get an idea of how we're doing in that area."

"I'm catching on now," said Gary. "First, we need to decide what our core values are; second, we need to develop a variety of ways to measure growth that reflects these values."

"You've got it," Jeff replied.

> "Therefore go and make disciples of all nations, baptizing
> them in the name of the Father and of the Son and of
> the Holy Spirit, and teaching them to obey everything I
> have commanded you. And surely I am with you always,
> to the very end of the age" (Matt. 28:19,20).

THE GIST OF IT...
WHY WE DO WHAT WE DO AND THE WAY WE DO IT

Quality improvement is more than doing things well. True quality is useless if it does not result in helping other people. If we are concerned with efficiency but not effectiveness, we'll be trying to improve things that do not make a difference.

Foolish expenditure of time, money and talents is far too common in a large number of churches today. Regardless of how well we're performing tasks, if we're not making a dent on lives for Kingdom purposes, we're wasting efforts.

That is why we must be about ministry effectiveness. When we put scarce money and talent into ministry that fails to build God's kingdom, we are running the risk of frustrating a demanding investor (see Matt. 25:14-30).

We assume that just keeping the church doors open and approximating last year's services is sufficient. More congregations and church leaders must ask questions on a regular basis, questions such as:

1. How are we doing?
2. Are we being effective?
3. If so, how do we know?
4. If not, why not?
5. If not, what are we willing to do to become more effective?

The Bible uses many forms of measurements, including groups of people, offerings, time and spiritual fruit. Because quality concerns all facets of ministry, we need not compromise.

QUESTIONS AND ANSWERS

Q. When we talk about spiritual vibrancy, where do we draw the line between feeding the saints and reaching the unchurched?

Alan: Different churches have different callings within God's kingdom. Some congregations are endowed with excellent evangelistic ministries, others with creative praise and worship, and still others with strong discipleship programs, but a healthy congregation needs all of these quality elements.

If we overemphasize outreach, we won't deepen our people once they make commitments. Like the seed that sprouted and then wilted for lack of roots, we'll lose people to other interests. If we overemphasize discipleship and Bible teaching, we'll stray from the Great Commission of reaching the world.

Sending money to foreign missions is a poor substitute for doing what is necessary to reach the unchurched next door. We need to do both. One way to look at balance is by reviewing budgets. Churches, like individuals, tend to reveal their hearts by where they place their treasures. When little money goes toward reaching others, the result is lopsided. If we claim we're investing in outreach but see few newcomers or even fewer converts, then we need to analyze the effectiveness of these ministries.

Stan: David Maister, the author of *True Professionalism: The Courage to Care About Your People, Your Clients*, denotes four key business principles in serving clients:

1. Ask your clients how to serve them better.
2. Invest heavily in your existing clients by demonstrating an interest in their affairs.
3. Design a package to demonstrate—not assert—that you have a special interest in them and have something of value to offer them.
4. Listen to your clients and discover their unique needs.

Any event conducted by a local church should be followed by moments of discussion and reflection. The formula offered by David Maister could easily be adapted by a local congregation to improve events offered to the public.

So let's keep focused on the goal, those of us who want everything that God has for us. If any of you have something else in mind, something less than total commitment, God will clear your blurred vision—you'll see it yet! (Phil. 3:14,15, *The Message*).

My brother, Mark, tells of the time he went into an ice cream store. There wasn't another customer in the place. He walked to the counter expecting to find a courteous clerk who would take his order. Instead of being greeted kindly, he was scolded and told to take a number and wait until his number was called, and he was the only customer in the store!

Have you ever felt that way? Have you ever felt that way at work? Have you ever attended a church and felt that way? We all have, but it doesn't have to be that way.

Q. Who do we listen to regarding who will shape the direction of our congregation?

Stan: George Gallup, Jr. says the seven basic needs of average Americans can become the basis for church ministry in the 1990s. Here is the result of that Gallup survey:

1. Food and shelter are basic necessities.
2. Seventy percent of survey respondents indicate they felt a need for purpose and meaning in their lives, but two-thirds of them thought churches were ineffective in meeting this need.
3. The need for relationships is evident since some 30 percent of Americans say they have been lonely for a long period during their lifetimes.
4. People need to feel appreciated and respected.
5. Laypeople want to be listened to, and the vast majority think the church's future should be determined more by the laity than the clergy.
6. People sense a need to grow spiritually.
7. People need to have practical assistance in reaching spiritual maturity.

In my opinion, we need to mesh the Gallup results with what our feedback tells us, then map out a strategy for a quality spiritual culture.

Alan: Churches, like families, tend to be full of opinions when it comes to getting things done. Going too many directions creates chaos, not quality. Place more emphasis on the secret shoppers and feedback from unchurched potential customers. They will reveal what you are or are not doing to connect with them. Most church environments are not seeker sensitive and tend to alienate those who are unfamiliar with a church culture.

Another concern is the people of influence who really do not understand the niche of the church. You often see people with money pushing pet ministry projects, trying to steer a church in a certain direction, regardless of what others think. This bullying can create havoc in the lives of a pastor and leadership team.

The goal is not to offend well-resourced people, but to engage them in a new vision and allow them to see how they can work together for mutual benefit. Although church leaders should not bow to the pressure of influential members, I see many shoot themselves in the feet by prematurely distancing themselves from people who may lack the right vision.

Q. This whole concept of measuring our spirituality sounds good, but it still sounds a bit nebulous. How can we quantify an intangible component like spiritual growth?

Alan: Our goal is not to make spirituality a scientific adventure. Ironically, a lot of the progress comes not in actually measuring spiritual growth, but in talking about and striving to measure it. Being held accountable for the spiritual quality in our church is the big idea behind church-quality improvement.

Jesus was upset with some of the churches mentioned in Revelation 2 and 3, which had a semblance of morality and religiosity but lacked the true, passionate heart that only comes by staying in touch with God's Spirit.

Pretending that everything is okay because you put in another year of programs and managed to cover the bills is hardly a quality affirmation. Taking a hard, honest look at ourselves and periodically seeking the advice of an outside consultant (paid professional or volunteer business leader) help us avoid game playing.

By now, we've all heard the stories of how the *R.M.S. Titanic* staff ignored the warnings of potential icebergs and went full speed ahead into their destruction. The problem is that when we keep steaming ahead, we assume we're doing just fine. We pat ourselves on the back for holding the fort one more year instead of storming the enemy's cache of goods. The benefit of wrestling with adequate standards is often in and of itself sufficient to uncover quality issues that need to be addressed.

Stan: Well stated, Alan. Prayer is the key to a great beginning. Enlist some prayer partners and pray for God's guidance and direction. Next, attempt to use the spiritual feedback to shape and develop your vision and values.

At Trinity, we came up with the idea of building a total quality spiritual culture based on Colossians 3:16,17:

> Let the Word of Christ—the Message—have the run of the house. Give it plenty of room in your lives. Instruct and direct one another using good common sense. And sing, sing your hearts out to God! Let every detail in your lives— words, actions, whatever—be done in the name of the Master, Jesus, thanking God the Father every step of the way *(The Message)*.

BUILDING A TOTAL QUALITY SPIRITUAL CULTURE AT TRINITY CHURCH OF THE NAZARENE

- Every believer has incredible potential.
- Everyone needs to be encouraged.
- Integrity in leadership is expected.
- An open-book policy is the norm.
- Kingdom-building will be the focus of every endeavor.
- Achievement by the laity will be appreciated and rewarded.
- All events will be done with excellence.
- God is the source of all good things.

After listening and understanding the feedback, the church must get on track, spiritually speaking. I recommend turning the focus to biblical models with your team leaders. Then look around for a good church model to follow. Most of all, trust God's sovereign guidance.

Q. It seems that one person can't be the sole catalyst for developing a spiritually vibrant congregation. What can a pastor or leadership team do to fire up a spiritually complacent congregation?

Stan: Preach teamwork! Great ministry teams pull together. Perhaps you've heard the story of a stranger walking down a residential street. He noticed a man struggling to get a washing machine through the doorway of his house.

When the stranger volunteered to help, the homeowner was overjoyed and the two men together began to work and struggle with the bulky appliance. After several minutes of fruitless effort, the two stopped and stared at each other in frustration. They looked on the verge of total exhaustion. Finally, when they had caught their breath, the stranger said to the homeowner, "We'll never get this washing machine in there."

To which the astonished homeowner replied, "Inside? I'm trying to move it out!"

Bottom line is that we have to cooperate in ministry endeavors. If we experience tension, I usually ask a levelheaded layperson to mediate the process and help us find points of agreement.

Alan: Even Jesus had his Judas. He left Nazareth for He could not do any miracles because of the people's disbelief. The Old Testament is full of examples of obstinate individuals who would not change even though change was necessary. Moses, Joshua and Caleb had their stubborn children of Israel. The unwillingness of the Israelites to change stopped them from entering into the rest of the Promised Land. The final result of such resistance is wandering.

As long as there is free will, there will be wandering. At times, leaders become sacrificial lambs in an effort to combat unbelief and stubbornness toward healthy change. Before leaving any situation, a leader should do his or her best to prepare the way for the successor by confronting issues that are confounding progress. A good exiting leader will pursue such changes regardless of whether he or she will be around to see the results.

Give people a taste of what they can have if they change directions. God has continually used a remnant to perpetuate His work and create change in a new generation. The remnant in your congregation may be small or large, but never underestimate the potential of a few people committed to seeing God do something new in their midst.

As a church grows, the pastor's hands-on ministry
must decrease and the congregation's hands-on
ministry must increase.

— C O N R A D   L O W E

THE DOERS SECTION

- In what areas of ministry are we doing a good job of analyzing quality improvement?
- What areas have we overlooked in our analysis?
- How can we ascertain the various spiritual levels of ministries offered in our church?
- How has this holistic approach to quality ministry review changed your thoughts about quality improvement in the context of the local church?

Ministry teamwork divides the task
and doubles the success.

— A L A N   N E L S O N

Chapter
13

The Learning Church

★ ★ ★ ★ ★

*All leaders are learners. The moment you stop
learning, you stop leading.*

— RICK WARREN

Two years passed quickly as Family Church implemented the
Initial Quality Improvement Training. On the eve of their two-year
anniversary, Jeff invited his friends Gary and Beth to meet him for
dinner at Capers. Amid the warm glow of candlelights, the rich
aroma of cooked meats and the soft sounds of music, Jeff applauded
his two friends. In a festive mood, he noted, "We have come a long
way since we began the training to become a five-star church!"

Jeff continued with a grin, "Both of you have done wonderfully
during the past two years of quarterly updates. The only thing on
the agenda for tonight is model the celebrating process. It's amazing
to see what has happened at Family Church."

"I know," Gary allowed. "I can't believe it either. There have
been more improvements in the last 24 months than probably in
anytime in our history. We've grown nearly 50 percent. I'm confident
that most, if not all of the growth, can be attributed to the significant
strides we've made in quality improvement."

Beth added, "I think a lot of it's been due to your leadership
Gary. As pastor, you've done a wonderful job of casting the vision."

"Thanks," said Gary, "but the people and the leadership team were much more responsive to the concepts than I originally thought they would be. And Beth, you've done a great job holding our feet to the fire. It's so easy to get back into the business-as-usual routine with everything else that needs to be done in a growing congregation."

"We now know that people want to pursue excellence," said Jeff. "They are attracted to quality. Obviously, our recent growth has shown that."

"What has amazed me is not only the growth," said Beth, "but also the sense of excitement and the new ministries that have begun because of our focus on improvement. You'd never know this had been a positive but sleepy church for so many years. We're awakening a giant."

"I think what we've discovered is that a quality improvement mind-set keeps you growing and changing as an organization," Jeff replied. "In Peter Senge's book about learning organizations, he makes it clear that to be effective in a changing world, we have to keep learning new ideas and new ways of doing business—or in our case, ministry. Churches in the past used to learn one way of doing things and stick with it. Cutting-edge churches now recognize that if they do the same, they'll soon become dinosaurs."

"Welcome to First Church of T-Rex," joked Beth.

Jeff laughed aloud and commented, "Too many churches are religious museums."

"Maybe so," Gary replied, "but we've become a learning church. Frequent training, leader lessons and ministry brainstorming have made us supple and flexible."

"And humble," Beth interjected. "People aren't as possessive of their ministries, and no one acts like they have all the answers."

"Humble is a good word for it," said Gary. "When you're in a learning mode, you don't get overconfident or proud that you've arrived. That's a good quality."

Jeff nodded. "It really is a fun way of doing church, isn't it?"

"Yeah," Gary agreed, "but it's also a great deal of work. We're always doing something new, something different, seeking feedback, and discussing better ways of ministry."

Jeff replied gleefully, "Kind of makes vacations more enjoyable though, doesn't it?"

"I've never been more fulfilled *and* more tired," Gary responded. "It's great! Most of my job has been lightened because each ministry team is operating its own ministry very well. Now most of my work is devoted to spending time with team directors. My wife is a happy camper, too. She sees more of me because I'm not the one running everyone else's ministry team."

Beth sighed, "Jeff, why don't more churches adopt this way of doing ministry? Why did it take us so long to incorporate quality improvement principles?"

"I think the biggest barrier is simply educational," said Jeff. "Most churches have not taken the time to figure out how quality improvement works in a ministry environment. You have done that."

"Thanks to you," said Beth.

"No, you came to me," Jeff reminded her. "I'm not as knowledgeable on church life as you are. But I think one reason churches have been slow to adopt such practices is because they are not forced to survive like most marketplace organizations."

"You may be right," Gary added, "but that is unfortunate."

"Right or wrong," Jeff explained, "people today are more quality minded and service oriented than ever before. If we don't raise the bar of excellence in all we do, we will go the way of many extinct businesses."

Gary sat back into his chair, sipped his coffee and replied, "I began thinking of quality improvement in terms of how it would grow and enhance our church, but now that we're in the middle of applying it, I'm thinking more of the theological reasons. First of all, God deserves our best. Giving Him our leftovers just isn't right. Since He's given us His best, how can we do anything less?"

"Whatever we do, we are to do it as to God," said Beth. "When we go to work, we need to do it with gusto. When we are with family and friends, we need to focus on them."

Gary elaborated, "A theology of excellence exists throughout the Bible, from character issues to the Ten Commandments to spiritual fruit and love. By giving our best, we glorify our Creator. When we do less than our best, we do not reflect His character."

"Gary and Beth," Jeff conceded, "I hope you know that over the last few months, you've taught me things about quality I've never considered, like being quality minded in all areas of my life," said Jeff. "We take a lot of effort at Majesty Suites to maintain our five-star rating, but I don't always do the same in other parts of my life, especially spiritually."

"Good point, Jeff," said Beth.

Silence fell among the group.

"Oh, one more thing," Jeff continued, as he pulled out a beautifully wrapped gift. "Here, this is for you, Gary."

Jeff handed the gift to Gary. Gary looked at Beth, surprised.

"What's this for, Jeff? I don't think it's my birthday."

"It's something else," Jeff replied.

Gary unwrapped the present and held up a beautifully engraved plaque. When he read the inscription, tears came to his eyes.

Beth was curious and asked, "What does it say, Gary?"

Gary handed the plaque to her.

Beth read the inscription out loud: "This is to award Family Church with the rating of *five stars* as a local congregation."

"Since there was no official agency to present this, I took the liberty," Jeff explained. "You both deserve this. Family Church has truly become a church that people love to attend. I'm proud to be associated with you and our community of faith."

Beth nodded agreement.

"Thank you, thank you so much, Jeff and Beth, for all your help," said Gary. "It's great to be a part of your ministry team."

The three friends hugged and celebrated their achievement, but no more than their Father, who smiled at what Family Church had become for His glory.

There are no victories at bargain prices.
—DWIGHT D. EISENHOWER

QUESTIONS AND ANSWERS

Q. How do we disseminate new ideas and training to our people so that we can become a learning congregation?

Alan: The future will see significant differences between the learners and the nonlearners. With information doubling every few years, we no longer have the option of relying on old knowledge. The Bible endures, but the methods of ministry that allow us to connect with people who need God and His Word are changing.

This requires us to be reading, attending conferences, brainstorming and networking ideas. The new way of ministry means constantly renewing ourselves with fresh ideas, cutting-edge concepts and implementing those we deem as helpful in our ministry.

Stan: Every pastor needs to have a strategy for learning and leadership. We need to be willing to ask the "what" questions:

What are our values?
What do we want to accomplish in our church?
What do we believe?
What is our role in the community?
What is the key to ministry effectiveness?

Q. How do we incorporate quality improvement as a part of our ongoing ministry preparation without it absorbing too much of our attention?

Stan: Peter Drucker once said, "Management by objectives works, if you know the objectives. Ninety percent of the time, you don't." Ouch!

I like the term "ministry by objectives." We must know where we are going. Jim Tignett, a key leader in the Hard Rock Cafe restaurant chain, made this observation: "Your restaurant stays hot as long as people hear about it, but they won't come back if the food isn't any good." Wow! As a learning church organization, we must constantly strive to present the "Bread of Life" in an effective manner.

Alan: You can gain a lot of steam for the ideas of ministry improvement and the pursuit of excellence by reading books like this and discussing them. Employing new ways of doing ministry involves change. The changes we're talking about here are not necessarily a specific type of music or preaching, but it's in how we do what we do.

Q. We've started to implement some of these ideas into our ministries. Where do we go from here? What's the next step after this book?

Alan: The Doers Section provides an implementation guide for your leadership team. You may want to have a separate ministry team look at quality issues in each ministry, but if you do this, you'll need to include all the ministry directors. If you don't, you'll receive resistance from some of them.

It is difficult for us to say specifically what you should do after going through the questions in The Doers Section. Every ministry is different. Each church is at a different point in their ministry, leadership, staffing and readiness. By using this book, however, your group will gain a good sense of where you need to head next.

Stan: In 1992, Paul Moyer, the pastor of First Presbyterian Church, Broadalbin, New York, brought nine key leaders to my Model Church Workshop in Boston, Massachusetts. Since that time, the key leaders have met every month as the Model Church Task Force.

Initially, they met resistance because it appeared they "knew something that no one else knew." Taking a cue from this experience, they began to enlighten the church through positive communication, verbal announcements and printed pieces. Today, they are a respected group of leaders who are responsible for guiding the vision and overall ministries of First Presbyterian Church.

Q. How do I know that this quality-improvement program will not be a passing fad?

Stan: The old saying, "Methods change, but principles never do" is correct. To me, we are dealing with a principle here.

Alan: The TQM (Total Quality Management) movement and subsequent generations of similar ideas continue to progress because the underlying concepts of quality are enduring. What tends to pass are terms, programs and gurus.

As long as quality and excellence are valued within our society, we as a church will need to be aware of them if we are to reach contemporary people.

If God deserves our best, then it is our responsibility to pursue it. Quality improvement may appear to be a fad when you get started, but the goal is for it to become an unconscious part of how you do ministry that continues in your future planning, staffing, training and practices.

Do that, and you and your congregation will become a five-star church!

Coming together is a beginning, staying together is progress, and working together is success.

—JAMES B. MILLER

THE DOERS SECTION

· What new ideas have been generated from the book that you might have included if you were writing additional chapters?
· What are some ideas that have been generated from your discussions that have already been implemented in your local church?
· What are the areas in which you would like to see significant quality improvement in your church?

- How has the process of teaching and training quality improvement been accepted?
- What do you need to release, in terms of your current time and ministry management, to make room for implementing a quality-improvement system?
- What can you do to make the process fun, instead of threatening and burdensome?
- Do you think your church has the potential to achieve a five-star church rating? If you were a part of an agency establishing this award, what standards of excellence would you require of churches?

The Secret Church Shopper Survey

★ ★ ★ ★ ★

The following is a possible checklist of items you would like the Church Shopper to observe and comment on in his or her feedback. Note that some of the items (i.e., nursery, youth department) may only be relevant if the shopper is a person needing that sort of ministry.

Facilities:

___ Parking (ease, accessibility, signage)
___ Ease in determining main entrance
___ Landscaping
___ Ease in finding the church
___ Exterior signs (condition, clarity, size)
___ Signage in finding where I need to go once inside
___ Exterior of facility and church buildings (paint, curb appeal)

Hospitality:

___ Greeting (by anyone, warmly/coolly, too gregarious)
___ Offered help in finding location/classroom
___ Appearance of greeters
___ Visible name badges
___ Offered bulletin/worship folder

____ Knowledgeable of facility/class locations/church information
____ Refreshments
____ Did I feel comfortable as a newcomer, or under a spotlight?

Nursery:
____ Signage/directions
____ Cleanliness
____ Staff (adequate number, competence, appearance)
____ Facility (size, appearance, equipment)
____ Check-in system
____ Security
____ Check-out system
____ Pager system

Children's:
____ Teacher there/semblance of order
____ I met the teacher
____ Child was greeted, made to feel at home
____ Directions to classroom
____ Introduction/orientation
____ Equipment
____ Decorations
____ Take-home materials
____ Check-in system
____ Check-out system
____ Follow-up

Youth:
____ Teacher there/semblance of order
____ I met the teacher
____ Youth was greeted, made to feel at home
____ Directions to classroom
____ Introduction/orientation
____ Equipment

___ Decorations
___ Follow-up

Worship Service:
___ Arrival time _____
___ Auditorium appearance
___ Seating (availability, comfort)
___ Help offered to find seat
___ Could I see the screen?
___ Could I follow the service items?
___ Was the music balanced (vocal versus instruments)?
___ Did the worship service flow freely?
___ Message/sermon
    ___ length
    ___ clarity
    ___ interest
    ___ relevance
    ___ notes
    ___ pastoral perceptions (attire, friendliness, etc.)
    ___ content
___ Audio (soft, loud, quality)
___ Friendliness (general feel, warmth)
___ Left understanding theme of the service?
___ Length of service
___ Relevance (contemporary, liturgical, traditional flavor)
___ Did I feel informed about what I was to do/when?

Rest Rooms:
___ Signage/directions
___ Lighting
___ Decor
___ Aroma
___ Cleanliness

Visual Image Package:
___ Bulletin/worship folder (printing, graphics, clarity, informative)
___ Newsletter
___ Brochures
___ Business card
___ Advertising
___ Logo
___ Signage
___ Foyer area
___ Information availability (arrangement, thoroughness, appeal)

Follow-Up:
___ Appropriate amount (too much, too little)
___ Type of follow-up received
___ Overall comfort (embarrassed, felt welcome, etc.)
___ Friendliness of people
___ Friendliness of pastor/staff

Miscellaneous Survey Possibilities:
___ Called the church for information and was received well.
___ Requests were followed-up by appropriate staff.
___ Received the information by mail in _____ days.
___ How is the church perceived in the community?
___ What are our strengths, weaknesses?
___ Is this a place where you would want to return? Why or why not?
___ Is this a place where you would invite your friends/neighbors to attend? Why or why not?

Church Rating Survey

★ ★ ★ ★ ★

Please rate us on a scale of one to five in the categories below:

1 = poor and signifies a ★ service rating
2 = mediocre and signifies a ★★ service rating
3 = average and signifies a ★★★ service rating
4 = good and signifies a ★★★★ service rating
5 = excellent and signifies a ★★★★★ service rating

1. Tonight I found the _____ event to be...

___ uplifting and fun
___ dull and uninspiring
___ just okay

2. The music/drama...

___ met a need in my life
___ was refreshing and useful
___ was just okay

3. The most meaningful moment for me was...

    __ prayer
    __ singing
    __ drama
    __ musical team

4. The amount of music was...

    __ too much
    __ too little
    __ just right

5. The visual aids/technology was...

    __ power point
    __ overhead slides
    __ event folder
    __ overall quality

6. Where were you first greeted...

in the parking lot?	❑ Yes	❑ No
at the church entrance?	❑ Yes	❑ No
in the sanctuary?	❑ Yes	❑ No

7. Did those seated near you at the event...

greet you before the program?	❑ Yes	❑ No
greet you during the fellowship time?	❑ Yes	❑ No
greet you after the event?	❑ Yes	❑ No

8. During my visit at _____ Church I felt...

   Please check any that apply:

❏ love	❏ apathy
❏ warmth	❏ coldness
❏ important	❏ unimportant
❏ happiness	❏ sadness
❏ acceptance	❏ loneliness
❏ enthusiasm	❏ indifference
❏ interest	❏ disinterest
❏ peace	❏ unrest

9. Were you able to easily locate...

visitor parking?	❏ Yes	❏ No	❏ N/A
nursery?	❏ Yes	❏ No	❏ N/A
rest room facilities?	❏ Yes	❏ No	❏ N/A
information central?	❏ Yes	❏ No	❏ N/A
visitor's booth?	❏ Yes	❏ No	❏ N/A
sanctuary?	❏ Yes	❏ No	❏ N/A

10. If you attended accompanied by children, please answer the following questions:

Did you feel comfortable leaving your child in the nursery?	❏ Yes	❏ No
Was a name tag placed on your child?	❏ Yes	❏ No
Was the teacher notified as to where to find parents if needed?	❏ Yes	❏ No

11. Did you experience anything negative   ❑ Yes   ❑ No
    that we should be aware of?

    If yes, please feel free to comment:

    _____

    _____

    _____

    _____

    _____

12. Overall, I would describe _____ as:

    ❑ extremely friendly   ❑ very friendly   ❑ friendly
    ❑ unfriendly   ❑ cold

A.C.T.S.
(Action/Contact Tracking System) Form

★ ★ ★ ★ ★

This is an interministry form used for quality communication and follow-up. The type used by one of the authors is printed on NCR triplicate stock, 5.5 x 8.5 inches, hole-punched for small, three-ring binder. A sample of the format is shown on the following page.

Church Name

A.C.T.S. Action/Contact Tracking System
Follow–Up Feedback for Ministry Excellence

(Please print or write legibly, providing adequate info for quality follow-through response. Thanks for caring!!)

Sender's Name & # _____ Date Sent/Given _____

Receiver/Responder _____ Please Respond By (Date) _____

Action/Contact Needed _____

_____

_____

Feedback/Response _____

_____

_____ Date of Feedback/Response _____

Sender/person seeking feedback gets white copy. Receiver gets yellow and pink. Receiver returns yellow with feedback to source and keeps pink.

Sample Agreements

✯ ✯ ✯ ✯ ✯

MINISTRY AGREEMENT AND EXPLANATION

Family Church Ministry Agreement (Sample)
Ministry Title: Kids Under Construction Teacher

Importance: "Jesus said, 'Let the little children come to me'" (Matt. 19:14). "Train up a child in the way he should go, and when he is old he will not depart from it" (Prov. 22:6, *NKJV*).

Description: The Kids Under Construction teacher is committed to teaching children about Jesus in formal and informal sessions. They will love and pray for and encourage kids to seek after God.

Responsible to: The Kids Under Construction Director(s), Teri Woodruff and Joanne Frazier.

Gifts/Skills: Teaching, a love for children, encouragement.

Responsibilities:

1. Preparation: Spend time as needed to prepare for a 30-to 40-minute, structured teaching time for a specific age group that might include a Bible lesson, game, craft, activity, Bible memory verse, sharing and prayer.

2. Before class: Arrive on Sunday one-half hour before service time for prayer, team building with the other teachers, and then set up the room before the service begins.

3. Class involvement: Spend time loving, encouraging and talking to each child. Start with an attention getter. Present a joyful, well-prepared, age-appropriate Bible lesson along with provided curriculum. Take an offering and pray. We ask teachers to prepare take-home papers. This will allow parents to know what the children are learning.

4. After class: Take a few moments to write in the "Teacher's Journal" as a way of connecting the class to next week's teacher. Take the Curriculum Book with you to "hand off" to the next teacher early in the week. Please know how the room was arranged and return it to its prior condition, cleaning furniture, storing supplies, etc., as we are guests of Laguna School and can lose our space if not cared for.

5. Parties: Work with your team teachers to plan class parties at least four times in the year.

6. Teacher's helpers: Keep in touch with your teacher's helpers. Involve them as much as you can. Many of these are teachers in training.

7. Substitutes: If you are unable to teach, it is your responsibility to trade with another team member. Please inform the Kids Under Construction director after you have found your replacement.

8. Prayer: Prayer is the difference between an average teacher and a special one. Pray for God's wisdom and that He will fill you with His love for the lesson and kids.

Estimated Time Commitment: Varies according to personal preparation time; approximately one to two hours of preparation outside of class per month, plus one hour per month for teaching and preclass community building, plus attending quarterly teacher/training meetings.

Budget: $5 per class reimbursement for copies, goodies, etc.

Training: Attend initial teaching training as well as quarterly training sessions as announced.

❏ Trial period: We understand that those who are new to teaching may find it beneficial to have a 90-day trial time, so that both teachers and directors can feel comfortable with a ministry match before a long-term commitment is entered into. (Please check this slot if appropriate.)

I agree to fulfill this ministry to the best of my ability through _____.

Print name_____

Signature_____

Date_____

(Record new date when the agreement is altered.)

_____ **Church Ministry Agreement (Format)**
Ministry Title: _____

Importance: (Scripture or biblical reference that gives the worker the role he/she has in God's kingdom and how the ministry fits into the big picture.)

Description: (One- or two-sentence overview of the ministry role.)

Responsible to: (Whomever the person should go to if there are concerns, questions.)

Gifts/skills: (Spiritual gifts, skills, aptitudes or interests that help a person know whether or not the position is right for him/her.)

Responsibilities: (A list of three to seven of the major tasks and expectations, without burdening down with too many specific instructions or information that is prone to change quickly. This helps the person get an overview of what is expected of him/her.)

Estimated time commitment: (This gives the participants an idea of how much time is required, how often they can expect to invest in ministry involvement and preparation.)

Budget: (How much money does the minister have available to spend with accountability?)

Training: (This includes initial orientation and training that will be provided, as well as continuing education.)

❏ Trial period: (This tends to be for first-time ministry participants who may not be sure whether or not the role fits him/her. This provides a handy "out" for both parties involved if role does not seem to fit the person.)

I agree to fulfill this ministry to the best of my ability through_____.

(You may want to provide a beginning and ending date. You may also want to begin all ministry agreements at the same time so that you know in advance when people should be reenlisting. This also avoids sporadic starting and stopping. The natural feel of many churches is the school year, September 1 through August 31, allowing a fresh fall start after the summer when recruiting and training can take place.)

Print name_____
Signature_____
Date _____

(Record new date when the agreement is altered.)

(One copy goes to the ministry director for his/her files and the other is kept by the participant for reference. This allows the director to hold the participant accountable according to the agreement and also helps the participant know what is and is not expected by the ministry director. The purpose is clear communication to enhance ministry involvement and quality participation.)

George Barna's Leadership Resources for the New Millennium

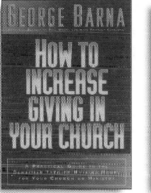

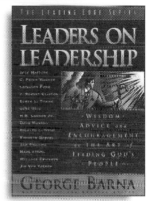

Evangelism that Works
How to Reach Changing Generations
with the Unchanging Gospel

George Barna

Paperback • 08307.17765

How to Increase Giving in Your Church
A Practical Guide to the Sensitive Task of
Raising Money for Your Church or Ministry

George Barna

Hardcover • 08307.18753
Video • 607135.000723

Leaders on Leadership
Wisdom, Advice andEncouragement
on the Art of Leading God's People

George Barna

Paperback • 08307.18621

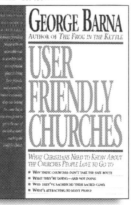

Turning Vision into Action
Defining and Putting into Practice the
Unique Vision God Has for Your Ministry

George Barna

Paperback • 08307.18664
Video • 607135.000754

User Friendly Churches
What Christians Need to Know About
the Churches People Love to Go To

George Barna

Paperback • 08307.14731

Generation Next
What You Need to Know About
Today's Youth

George Barna

Paperback • 0185240.18095

Available at your local Christian bookstore.

Regal
FROM GOSPEL LIGHT

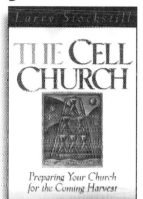
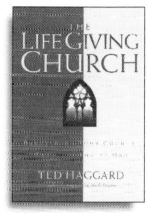
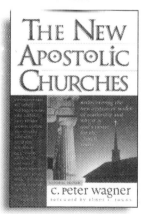

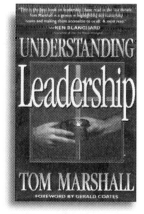